Indian

Attia Hosain

Hamlyn Paperbacks

INDIAN COOKING
ISBN 0 600 32036 7

First published in Great Britain 1963
by Paul Hamlyn Ltd
Second edition published 1969
Revised edition published 1981

Hamlyn Paperbacks are published by
The Hamlyn Publishing Group Ltd,
Astronaut House,
Feltham, Middlesex, England
(Paperback Division: Hamlyn Paperbacks,
Banda House, Cambridge Grove,
Hammersmith, London W6 0LE)

Printed and bound in Great Britain by
Cox & Wyman Ltd, Reading

Contents

Useful Facts and Figures

Notes on metrication

In this book quantities are given in metric and Imperial measures. Exact conversion from Imperial to metric measures does not usually give very convenient working quantities and so the metric measures have been rounded off into units of 25 grams. The table below shows the recommended equivalents.

Ounces	*Approx g to nearest whole figure*	*Recommended conversion to nearest unit of 25*
1	28	25
2	57	50
3	85	75
4	113	100
5	142	150
6	170	175
7	198	200
8	227	225
9	255	250
10	283	275
11	312	300
12	340	350
13	368	375
14	396	400
15	425	425
16 (1 lb)	454	450
17	482	475
18	510	500
19	539	550
20 (1¼ lb)	567	575

Note: When converting quantities over 20 oz first add the appropriate figures in the centre column, then adjust to the nearest unit of 25. As a general guide, 1 kg (1000 g) equals 2.2 lb or about 2 lb 3 oz. This method of conversion gives good results in nearly all cases, although in certain pastry and cake recipes a more accurate conversion is necessary.

Liquid measures The millilitre has been used in this book and the following table gives a few examples.

Imperial	*Approx ml to nearest whole figure*	*Recommended ml*
¼ pint	142	150 ml
½ pint	283	300 ml
¾ pint	425	450 ml
1 pint	567	600 ml
1½ pints	851	900 ml
1¾ pints	992	1000 ml (1 litre)

Spoon measures All spoon measures given in this book are level unless otherwise stated.

Can sizes At present, cans are marked with the exact (usually to the nearest whole number) metric equivalent of the Imperial weight of the contents, so we have followed this practice when giving can sizes.

Oven temperatures

The table below gives recommended equivalents.

	°C	*°F*	*Gas Mark*
Very cool	110	225	¼
	120	250	½
Cool	140	275	1
	150	300	2
Moderate	160	325	3
	180	350	4
Moderately hot	190	375	5
	200	400	6
Hot	220	425	7
	230	450	8
Very hot	240	475	9

Notes for American and Australian users

In America the 8-oz measuring cup is used. In Australia metric measures are now used in conjunction with the standard 250-ml measuring cup. The Imperial pint, used in Britain and Australia, is 20 fl oz, while the American pint is 16 fl oz. It is important to remember that the Australian tablespoon differs from both the British and American tablespoons; the table below gives a comparison. The British standard tablespoon, which has been used throughout this book, holds 17.7 ml, the American 14.2 ml, and the Australian 20 ml. A teaspoon holds approximately 5 ml in all three countries.

British	*American*	*Australian*
1 teaspoon	1 teaspoon	1 teaspoon
1 tablespoon	1 tablespoon	1 tablespoon
2 tablespoons	3 tablespoons	2 tablespoons
3½ tablespoons	4 tablespoons	3 tablespoons
4 tablespoons	5 tablespoons	3½ tablespoons

An Imperial/American guide to solid and liquid measures

Solid measures

IMPERIAL	AMERICAN
1 lb butter or margarine	2 cups
1 lb flour	4 cups
1 lb granulated or castor sugar	2 cups
1 lb icing sugar	3 cups
8 oz rice	1 cup

Liquid measures

IMPERIAL	AMERICAN
¼ pint liquid	⅔ cup liquid
½ pint	1¼ cups
¾ pint	2 cups
1 pint	2½ cups
1½ pints	3¾ cups
2 pints	5 cups (2½ pints)

Note **When making any of the recipes in this book, only follow one set of measures as they are not interchangeable.**

Introduction

The eating habits of a people are largely influenced by historical and geographical factors, which in their turn influence customs and social behaviour.

The Indo-Pakistan sub-continent presents an extremely complex pattern of life because of the many different races with different religions that form its population. Since the earliest times, throughout the centuries, there were repeated invasions from the north. Aryans, Greeks and Moguls came into this rich land through the mountain passes and most of the invaders stayed to make the sub-continent their home — except the Europeans who came in later years to trade, stayed to rule and left when the sub-continent was divided into the two independent countries of India and Pakistan.

The influence of all these different races is to be found in the culture and consequently in the eating habits of the people of the sub-continent. Indian food is therefore no different from Pakistani food, depending on the influences which are predominant in any particular region.

Thus we see that the northern portions of India and Pakistan have been greatly influenced by the diet of central Asia through the Mogul invaders who came from there. Such common words as Kabab, Keema and Pulao (Pilaff) bear witness to this.

Again, religious beliefs have had their impact. The eating of beef is forbidden to the Hindu, and the eating of the pig and its derivatives to Muslims. A large section of the population do not eat meat in any form. This has largely been brought about by the influence of Buddhism and allied schools of thought, which teach an abhorrence of the taking of life.

Nevertheless, there is a common element amongst all the foods on the sub-continent and that is the use of condiments and spices to a greater extent than in Europe. This is not surprising considering that this part of the world is the historical home of the exotic spices which were such a large and lucrative item of trade for Europe during the Middle Ages and even earlier. It was the quest for these spices that led to the discovery of the New World and the subsequent opening up of geographical frontiers throughout the world.

In India the use of spices is generally greater the further southwards one goes. Apart from other factors, this is undoubtedly because in humid climates spices preserve food and stimulate jaded appetites. The highly spiced hot Madras curries or the well known Madrassi Soup, Mulligatawny, are very different from the grilled meat of northern areas, the Tikka Kebabs and Tandoori Murgh, spiced only with pepper, salt and a little garlic.

But food changed from its simpler forms into more and more complicated ones as social changes were brought about by material and cultural progress.

The art of the presentation of food was developed. Silver or gold leaf is used as a decoration for various dishes. The metal is beaten so fine that it can be blown away by a breath. Cooks also vied with each other to produce strange new dishes and camouflage the materials used. Even now the tradition remains. For example, it is possible to eat what you believe to be a fish curry only to learn afterwards that it was made from unripe bananas, or to taste a sweet Halva and find it to have been made not of fruit or vegetables but meat.

There is no special order in which an Indian meal is served, no separate courses, except that sweet dishes are served last. Curries, their accompaniments, chutneys and pickles are served together and eaten with rice and chapatis.

Second helpings are quite in order; therefore it seems strange when people newly introduced to Indian food pile up their plates in a way they would never dream of doing with their own food.

Most people in India serve food in small metal bowls arranged in a round tray or metal thali. These are of brass, stainless steel or silver and each person has his own thali. Or the food is placed in the centre and served on individual plates.

The traditional Indian style of eating is with the fingers, and contrary to the impression which most people who do not know about the conventions have, this has to be done with great fastidiousness. Hands are carefully washed before and after meals, and it is customary to rinse the mouth after every meal.

Western ways of living have been absorbed into Indian ways, and in many houses tables are laid and crockery and cutlery are used in the same way as in the West. Often one or two European dishes are served together with Indian food.

After a meal, it is usual to serve pan (betel leaf) or nuts, aniseed and cardamom. Tea and green tea are served in the north and coffee in the south.

All recipes are meant to serve four people at least; the qualification is deliberate. One of the virtues of Indian food is that an unexpected guest need cause no panic or embarrassment; there is always food for the extra guest or two. Perhaps this is one of the most important reasons for our traditional hospitality. Just as one can more easily increase the quantity of a stew or a goulash it is easier to make a curry or dish of lentils go further than just so many steaks or chops or slices of meat.

We have given weights and measures of ingredients, but please consider these as indications of the quantities that should be used, and do not be afraid to experiment once you have become familiar with the technique of cooking dishes that sound strange and exotic.

Good cooks never really know exactly how much of this or that they have used. There is no substitute for the sense of taste. This is particularly true of salt, pepper and chilli. One can never really tell how much to use; it depends very much on individual taste.

Remember that a curry need not necessarily be 'hot', and spices can be used in varying combinations, using more of one and less of another as one wishes, depending on the flavour and 'scent' one prefers.

As far as possible the recipes in this book have been chosen with the problems of housewives abroad in mind. We have these problems ourselves and can appreciate them. Some of the recipes are elaborate, but most have been made as simple as possible.

The important thing to remember is that the less water used and the slower the cooking the better the taste of the food because the spices can be absorbed. That is why Indian food seems to improve when left-overs are reheated.

If a particular recipe requires the use of water or liquid, it should be brought to the boil and the heat lowered to simmering point till cooked.

It is impossible to give the cooking time for every recipe. So much depends on the quality of the meat or vegetables being cooked. It depends on when the meat is tender and the vegetables soft, and this can be found out only by practical tests.

If a pressure cooker is used, then, after the meat is tender, keep cooking on a medium heat, without the lid, till the surplus water has been absorbed.

Some of the most delicious and elaborate dishes are cooked in India with primitive utensils on improvised brick stoves and in baked mud ovens.

Unless otherwise stated all spices are meant to be used in powdered form. These can be bought in tins or by weight. The best flavour is, of course, obtained from fresh spices, freshly ground with a mortar and pestle, on a grindstone or in an electric grinder. All the ingredients are available in shops and stores that stock Indian groceries.

We should like to acknowledge our debt to Mrs Dina Khareghat in helping us. Her experience and knowledge have been invaluable.

Glossary of Indian Words

SPICES AND CONDIMENTS

Aniseed	*Saunf*
Asafoetida	*Heeng*
Bay leaf	*Tej patta*
Cardamom	*Ilaichi*
Chilli	*Mirch*
Cinnamon	*Dalchini*
Cloves	*Laung*
Coriander	*Dhaniya*
Cummin	*Zeera*
Fenugreek	*Methi*
Garlic	*Lehsun*
Ginger	*Adrak*
Mace	*Javitri*
Mint	*Podina*
Mustard	*Sarson*
Nutmeg	*Jaiphal*
Onion seeds	*Kalaunji*
Parsley	*Ajmoda ke patte*
Peppercorns	*Kali mirch*
Pomegranate seeds	*Anardana*
Poppy seeds	*Khaskhas*
Saffron	*Zafran or Kesar*
Sesame	*Til*
Tamarind	*Imli*
Turmeric	*Haldi*

FRUIT, VEGETABLES AND NUTS

Aubergines	*Brinjal or Baigan*
Almonds	*Badam*
Apples	*Seb*
Apricots	*Khubani*
Banana	*Kela*
Beetroot	*Chukander*
Broad beans	*Sem*
Cabbage	*Bund gobhi*
Carrot	*Gajar*
Cashew nut	*Kaju*
Cauliflower	*Phool gobhi*

Fig	*Anjeer*
Gourd	*Kerala*
Grape	*Angoor*
Groundnuts	*Moongphali*
Lemon	*Neembu*
Mango	*Aam*
Okra	*Bhindi*
Olives	*Zaitun*
Onions	*Piaz*
Orange	*Narangi*
Peaches	*Aaru*
Peas	*Mattar*
Pepper, green (Capsicum)	*Bari mirch*
Pineapple	*Ananas*
Potatoes	*Aloo*
Pumpkin	*Kaddu*
Radish	*Mooli*
Raisins	*Kishmish*
Sweet potato	*Shakarkand*
Tomato	*Tamatar*
Turnip	*Shalgam*
Walnut	*Akhrot*

PULSES AND FLOURS

Black-eyed beans	*Lobia*
Chick peas	*Chana or Gram dal*
Chick pea flour	*Gram or Besan*
Flour	*Maida*
Lentils	*Masoor or Urad dal*
Millet	*Bajra*
Mung beans	*Mung dal*
Pigeon peas	*Arhar or Tuar dal*
Semolina	*Sooji*
Wholemeal flour	*Atta*

MISCELLANEOUS

Brains	*Bheja*
Butter	*Makkhan*
Chicken	*Murghi*
Coconut	*Narial*
Curd	*Dahi*

Duck	*Bathak; Murghabi*
Eggs	*Ande*
Fish	*Machli*
Kidney	*Gurda*
Liver	*Kaleji*
Meat	*Gosht*
Mince	*Keema*
Mustard oil	*Sarson ka tel*
Olive oil	*Zaitun ka tel*
Pheasant	*Titar*
Prawns	*Jheengé*
Pulses	*Dal*
Quail	*Batér*
Sugar	*Shakar*
Sweets	*Mithai*
Vermicelli	*Sevain*
Vegetables	*Tarkari*
Vinegar	*Sirka*
Yogurt	*Dahi*

Basic Cooking Materials

As a general rule it is considered best to cook with clarified butter (ghee). But mechanically prepared hydrogenated vegetable fats, which are cheaper, have now come to be used by most people.

Of vegetable oils mustard oil is by far the most popular. This has a pungent flavour and is particularly suitable for the cooking of fish and vegetables after it has reached a high temperature. Modern science indicates that oils are far more suitable for cooking than butter because they have little or no cholesterol-forming contents.

In most of the recipes given in this book no specific fat or oil is mentioned, because almost any medium can be used depending on individual choice. Lard, however, is not used for Indian cooking.

GRAM FLOUR

Gram or besan is the flour made from chana dal. This can be bought at any shop selling Indian groceries. If it is not available then the following substitute can be used:

Roast chick peas or yellow split peas in a heavy pan, being careful to turn constantly so as to prevent burning. Cool. Grind in an electric grinder, or using a mortar and pestle, as fine as possible. Put through a fine sieve. Store in a tightly covered jar.

GHEE

The best way to make ghee is to place the desired quantity of butter in a saucepan and allow to simmer without burning for at least 1½ to 2 hours. After removing from the heat, strain through fine muslin. Store in a jar. Margarine can be clarified in the same way.

GARAM MASALA

METRIC/IMPERIAL

225 g/8 oz coriander seeds
225 g/8 oz cummin seeds
100 g/4 oz large cardamoms
50 g/2 oz ground cinnamon
100 g/4 oz peppercorns
50 g/2 oz cloves
1 teaspoon grated nutmeg

Roast the coriander and cummin seeds separately. Peel the cardamoms. Grind all the spices, add the grated nutmeg and store in an airtight container. Use as directed in recipes. Garam masala can be obtained from shops selling Indian groceries.

YOGURT
(Dahi)

To make yogurt for the first time you will require a small (142-g/5-oz) carton of yogurt. Bring 600 ml/1 pint of milk to the boil and remove from the heat. Put into a wide-mouthed bottle or a bowl and cool to blood heat. Add a tablespoonful of yogurt and mix thoroughly. Cover and keep in a warm place till it sets. Use when quite cold. Once you have made the yogurt, always keep a little to start the next lot.

In India yogurt is considered very beneficial to health and is eaten extensively both as a savoury and as a sweet. To make sweet yogurt, add sugar to the milk before boiling.

COCONUT MILK

METRIC/IMPERIAL

50 g/2 oz coconut cream or desiccated coconut
150 ml/¼ pint hot water

Dissolve coconut in the hot water. This makes a thick mixture. More or less water can be added according to taste.

PANIR
(Cheese)

METRIC/IMPERIAL

generous litre/2 pints milk   juice of 1 lemon

Boil the milk and add lemon juice. Stir and when the milk curdles remove from the heat. Strain into a piece of muslin but keep the whey. Hang the cheese till all the water has dripped. Do not squeeze but allow to drip overnight.

Put the cheese under a weight so that it becomes flat and all the moisture is removed.

TAMARIND WATER

METRIC/IMPERIAL

lump of tamarind (walnut size)   150 ml/¼ pint hot water

Soak tamarind in hot water. When cool (approximately 10 minutes) squeeze and strain the water into a cup. If a more sour taste is required then more tamarind can be used.

The juice of 2 lemons or 6 tablespoons strong vinegar is equal to the above tamarind preparation.

Sometimes sugar or gur (Indian molasses) is dissolved in tamarind water to give a sweet and sour taste.

GINGER, GARLIC OR ONION JUICE

To extract green ginger, garlic or onion juices, pound the required condiment in a mortar after peeling it. Add 2 teaspoons of water while pounding. Then put water and condiment in a clean muslin and squeeze the juice. Put the squeezed condiment back in the mortar, add 1 teaspoon of water and pound again. Squeeze condiment and water again through muslin into first amount of juice. The juice will now be ready for use as desired. If onion is used, chop coarsely first before pounding.

Bread

In its simplest form the flat unleavened bread eaten on the sub-continent is called chapati. In appearance it resembles tortilla. It has many variations: the thick, coarse type is called roti, while the refined varieties, light and thin in texture, are known as phulkas and chapatis. The lighter and larger the chapati, the better the cook.

There are other forms of bread too, fried and baked. Puris are deep fried, puffed and light. Parathas are heavier, shallow fried, either plain or stuffed.

All dishes, except the sweet course, are eaten with bread and rice, but bread and rice are never eaten together. Whether bread or rice is eaten first depends on the custom prevailing in any particular place. Where rice is a delicacy it is usually eaten first.

All forms of Indian bread must be served piping hot.

CHAPATIS
(Wholemeal Bread)

METRIC/IMPERIAL

450 g/1 lb wholemeal flour
cold water
butter

Mix flour and sufficient water to make a fairly stiff dough. Knead very thoroughly, using a little more water to make a pliable dough. Cover with a damp cloth and leave for 2 or 3 hours. Knead again. Take pieces as large as an egg and make into round balls. Flatten the balls and roll out very thinly into rounds the size of a small plate. Heat griddle till it is very hot and put a chapati on it for about 15 seconds, then turn the chapati and cook till brown spots appear; turn it over and press gently on the sides with a clean cloth till the chapati puffs up. Take off the griddle, butter on one side only and serve. To keep soft and hot wrap the chapatis in a clean cloth.

All chapatis should be served hot and preferably as soon as they are cooked.

PLAIN FLOUR CHAPATIS

METRIC/IMPERIAL

350 g/12 oz plain flour
2 teaspoons salt
90 g/3½ oz butter
cold water
50 g/2 oz melted butter

Sift the flour and salt together into a bowl and add 40 g/1½ oz butter cut in small pieces. Blend in with pastry blender till mixture is consistency of breadcrumbs. Add just enough cold water to knead into a soft dough. Divide into 8 parts. Take one part of the dough and roll out round like a small plate. Brush with melted butter, dust with flour and roll up into a ball again. Do this twice more. Now roll each ball into a flat chapati. Heat griddle till it is very hot and put the chapatis on it one at a time. Cook for 1 minute each side. Then brush round the edge with melted butter and fry, turning, till both sides are brown and crisp. Lower the heat under the griddle once the frying starts, but see that the griddle is white hot for each new chapati.

GRAM FLOUR CHAPATIS

METRIC/IMPERIAL

1 onion
¼ green pepper
1 tablespoon coriander or watercress leaves
100 g/4 oz gram or wholewheat flour
175 g/6 oz plain flour
1 teaspoon salt
cold water
25 g/1 oz cooking fat

Slice the peeled onion thinly, mince the pepper and coriander or watercress leaves finely. Sift the gram or wholewheat flour, white flour and salt together. Then mix well with the onion and minced leaves and pepper. Use as much ice cold water as required to make a soft dough. Divide it up into small walnut size balls. Flatten and roll out into the size of a small plate. Heat the griddle till it is very hot, brush it with cooking fat and cook the chapatis (they should be like thick pancakes) on both sides till brown in colour and cooked through.

MILK CHAPATIS

METRIC/IMPERIAL

450 g/1 lb plain flour
salt
25 g/1 oz butter
3 tablespoons milk
cold water

Sift the flour and salt together. Blend in the butter, then knead the whole to a soft dough with the milk and as much cold water as required. Divide into 16 parts and roll out each part to 5 mm/¼ inch thick. Heat the griddle till it is very hot, lower heat and heat gently until nicely cooked, brown and crisp.

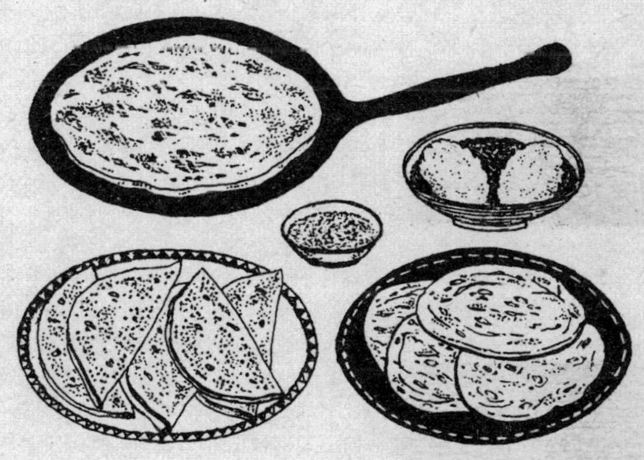

CHAPATI IN LAYERS

METRIC/IMPERIAL

450 g/1 lb plain flour
3 teaspoons salt
3 tablespoons milk
(use more if needed)
50 g/2 oz butter
50 g/2 oz butter for frying

Sift the flour and salt together. Then add the milk and butter and knead to a soft dough. Divide the dough into three equal parts. Roll out into large thin chapatis of equal size. Brush one with butter and sprinkle with dry flour. Place the second chapati on the first, brush with butter and sprinkle with dry flour. Place the third chapati on the second and press down lightly. Heat the griddle till very hot and fry the chapati, brushing with butter often and turning constantly. Lower the heat when frying or the chapati will not be cooked through. When ready cut in four and serve hot.

CHAPATI BALLS

METRIC/IMPERIAL

225 g/8 oz urad dal	15 g/½ oz cooking fat or butter
½ teaspoon garam masala	225 g/8 oz plain flour
¼ teaspoon chilli powder	2 teaspoons salt
½ teaspoon cummin powder	15 g/½ oz butter
1 teaspoon salt	cold water

Soak the urad dal in water that just covers it. Then in the same water bring it to the boil and simmer till the dal is quite soft and can be mashed. Mash it all and add the garam masala, chilli, cummin and salt and mix well with the dal. Then heat cooking fat in a frying pan and fry the dal mixture till dry. Sift together flour and 2 teaspoons salt and cut in butter. Then add enough cold water to make a soft dough and knead well. The dough must be very soft. Divide into 8 parts. Make into balls. Depress each ball and fill with the dal filling that has been fried dry. Close up ball and flatten out as wide as possible without breaking into the filling. Fry the cakes gently on both sides till done. Use more butter for frying if needed.

PARATHA

METRIC/IMPERIAL

450 g/1 lb wholemeal flour	melted ghee or butter

Make a dough as for chapati. Roll into rounds and brush with melted ghee. Fold in half and press the edges. Brush with ghee and fold again. Roll into fan shapes and cook on a hot griddle, turning the bread three times. Brush a little ghee round the edges of the paratha. It should swell up. Turn and fry the other side (½ teaspoon ghee is enough for frying both sides). Remove and serve hot.

STUFFED PARATHAS

METRIC/IMPERIAL

100 g/4 oz plain flour
1 teaspoon salt
50 g/2 oz butter
cold water
root horseradish

Sift the flour and salt together. Blend in 15 g/½ oz of the butter and make into a soft dough with cold water. Divide into 8 parts. Roll out each piece thinly to a round shape. Grate the horseradish. Spread the horseradish on one round and cover with another. Make four stuffed parathas all together. Heat the griddle till very hot and fry the parathas in the rest of the butter. Lower heat and cook gently. Any mashed, boiled or grated vegetables can be used instead of horseradish.

ALU KI ROTI
(Parathas with Potato Stuffing)

METRIC/IMPERIAL

225 g/8 oz potatoes
450 g/1 lb wholemeal flour
water
1 onion
2 green chillies
¼ teaspoon ginger powder
salt to taste
100 g/4 oz ghee or butter

Boil and mash the potatoes. Cool. Make a dough with flour and water. Knead well till it is soft and pliable. Cover with a damp cloth and leave for 1 hour.

Chop the onion and green chillies very finely. Add to the potatoes with the ginger and salt. Melt the fat in a small pan and keep warm. Take a piece of dough the size of a large plum and make into a ball; flatten a little, brush with the fat and put 2 teaspoons of the potato in the centre. Cover the potato by drawing up the edges towards the centre. Press the cake on a floured board and roll out into a round as large as a saucer. Put the paratha on a hot griddle, cook for 1 minute, turn and after another minute add a very little fat to the edges. Turn again and when brown patches appear on both sides the paratha is ready.

ROGNI ROTI

METRIC/IMPERIAL

450 g/1 lb wholemeal flour
50 g/2 oz cream
salt to taste
150 ml/¼ pint milk
50 g/2 oz ghee

Sift flour and add the cream, salt, milk and ghee. Knead the dough till soft and pliable. Make balls the size of a large egg and roll into rounds the size of a small plate. Cook on a very hot griddle, like chapati.

POORI

METRIC/IMPERIAL

450 g/1 lb wholemeal flour
water
vegetable fat for frying

Knead flour with water to make a soft pliable dough. Keep covered with a damp cloth for an hour or so. Knead again till the dough is smooth and does not stick to the hands. Make small balls the size of an egg. Roll these out on a floured board till they are the size of a small saucer. Put the fat in a deep frying pan and when smoking hot put in one poori at a time. With a flat spoon press the poori gently till it puffs out; turn and cook till pale gold. Drain and keep hot or serve at once.

SEMOLINA POORIS

METRIC/IMPERIAL

225 g/8 oz plain flour
100 g/4 oz semolina
½ teaspoon turmeric
1½ teaspoons salt
40 g/1½ oz butter
cold water
25 g/1 oz rice flour
25 g/1 oz fat for frying

Mix the plain flour, semolina, turmeric and salt. Then add 25 g/1 oz of the butter in little pieces and blend with a pastry blender in a bowl till it is like sand. Form into a soft dough with the help of cold water, kneading the dough well. Now add the remaining butter to the rice flour and beat with rotary beater till creamy. Roll out the soft dough into a large circle and spread the rice flour mixture evenly on it. Roll it up and roll out again. Cut into largish rounds with a biscuit cutter and fry in the heated fat in the frying pan. Use oil or butter as liked, but the fat must be hot. Serve at once.

COCONUT BREAD

METRIC/IMPERIAL

2 tablespoons desiccated coconut
1 teaspoon salt
3 tablespoons plain flour
pinch of cayenne pepper
½ teaspoon sugar
cold water
50 g/2 oz cooking fat

Mix all the dry ingredients together and form a soft dough with cold water. Roll out into small flat cakes. Fry them a few at a time in the heated cooking fat in a frying pan till cooked and lightish brown.

DOSA
(Stuffed Pancakes from Southern India)

METRIC/IMPERIAL

225 g/8 oz rice
100 g/4 oz urad dal
salt to taste
cold water
ghee or oil

Wash rice and dal and soak separately overnight. Drain and when dry grind each separately. Add salt to the rice and add the dal. With cold water make into a medium batter neither too thick nor too thin. Heat a frying pan and put in a little ghee to grease the pan. When smoking, put in enough batter to cover the bottom of the pan. Cook both sides of the pancake and remove.

Serve with chutneys or with special potato bhaji (see below) used for stuffing the dosa.

POTATO BHAJI
(Stuffing for Dosa)

METRIC/IMPERIAL

225 g/8 oz potatoes
1 medium onion
25 g/1 oz ghee
¼ teaspoon mustard seeds
¼ teaspoon turmeric
¼ teaspoon chilli powder
salt and pepper

Boil the potatoes. Peel and dice them. Chop the onion finely. Heat the ghee and fry the mustard seeds. Add the onion and fry till just softened. Add potatoes, turmeric, chilli and salt. Cook for 5 minutes till dry. Add pepper.

Put a spoonful of the above in the centre of each dosa and serve.

DOSA
(Another Method)

METRIC/IMPERIAL

175 g/6 oz rice flour
175 g/6 oz plain flour
salt to taste
2 tablespoons yogurt
1 tablespoon ghee
a little chilli powder (optional)
water

Mix the rice flour with the plain flour. Add salt, yogurt, ghee, chilli and enough water to make a thick batter. Keep overnight to ferment. Cook in a pan like an omelette. Serve hot with vegetables or meat curry.

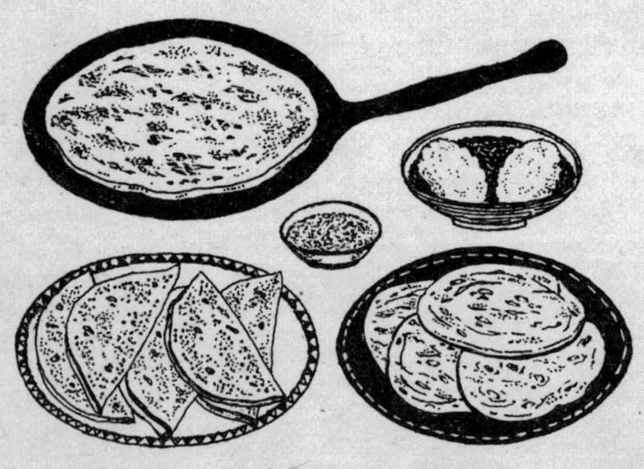

Rice

Rice is the staple diet in the south and east, the main rice-growing areas of India. Like bread, it is used as a basis of the meal, and its cooking has been developed to a fine art, from the simplest boiled form to the most elaborate and highly spiced biryanis.

Many different varieties of rice grain are used: unpolished, long and short grain, rice matured over many years, rice from the current harvest. Every variety has different cooking characteristics, therefore the satisfactory cooking of rice cannot be learned merely from recipes. Several methods of boiling and frying rice are given in this section, but a certain amount of trial and error is necessary to get the best in any particular place. If overcooked or stirred too much rice becomes mushy. It is best to use a heavy pan.

PLAIN BOILED RICE (1)

Oven temperature: Very cool
120°C, 250°F, Gas Mark ½

METRIC/IMPERIAL

450 g/1 lb rice	3.5 litres/6 pints water

Wash rice thoroughly and drain. Put in a saucepan with the water and bring to the boil. Take the lid off and boil fairly briskly for 15 to 20 minutes. To test whether the rice is cooked, take one or two grains and rub between the finger and thumb: if cooked there should be no granules. Drain rice in a colander and place colander over a saucepan containing hot water. Put this over a low heat till the rice is dry. The rice should be covered while steaming. Alternatively, the rice can be put in an ovenproof dish after draining and put in the oven for 10 or 15 minutes.

PLAIN BOILED RICE (2)

METRIC/IMPERIAL

450 g/1 lb rice
3.5 litres/6 pints water
2 teaspoons salt

Wash rice thoroughly and drain. Put it into the boiling salted water and boil fairly briskly for 15 or 20 minutes. To test whether the rice is cooked, take one or two grains and rub between finger and thumb; if cooked, there should be no granules. Drain the rice in a colander and finish as for Plain Boiled Rice (1).

PLAIN BOILED RICE (3)

METRIC/IMPERIAL

450 g/1 lb rice
generous litre/2 pints water

Wash rice thoroughly and drain. Put the rice into a large saucepan and add cold water. Bring to the boil over medium heat. When the water starts boiling cover the saucepan with a damp teacloth and put the lid on. This is to ensure that no steam evaporates. Turn the heat very low and simmer for 20 minutes without removing cloth. After 20 minutes you will find that the rice is cooked and each grain separate.

SIMPLE FRIED RICE (1)

Oven temperature: Very cool
120°C, 250°F, Gas Mark ½

METRIC/IMPERIAL

100 g/4 oz ghee or butter
450 g/1 lb rice
2 teaspoons salt
scant 1.5 litres/2½ pints water

Heat the fat and add the rice, which should be washed and drained. Add the salt and keep stirring till the rice appears glazed. Add boiling water and bring to the boil. Simmer until the water is nearly all absorbed. Put in the oven for about 20 minutes, when the rice should be ready.

If the saucepan will not fit into the oven, turn the half cooked rice into an ovenproof dish and put in the oven. The dish should be covered.

FRIED RICE (2)

Oven temperature: Very cool
120°C, 250°F, Gas Mark ½

METRIC/IMPERIAL

100 g/4 oz ghee or butter
1 onion
450 g/1 lb rice
1 small stick cinnamon
1 bay leaf
3 peppercorns
2 teaspoons salt

Heat the ghee in a large saucepan and add the finely sliced onion. Fry till golden brown, remove from the pan and keep aside. To the hot fat add the washed and drained rice and the spices. Keep stirring and fry for 4 or 5 minutes till the rice appears glazed. Now add salt and boiling water. The water should come to 2.5 cm/1 inch above the rice. Bring to the boil and simmer gently till the water is nearly all absorbed. Put in the oven and leave for 20 or 25 minutes till the rice is cooked. Serve garnished with fried onions or hard-boiled eggs cut in slices.

FRIED RICE PARSEE STYLE

Oven temperature: Very cool
120°C, 250°F, Gas Mark ½

METRIC/IMPERIAL

450 g/1 lb rice
2 large onions
4 green cardamoms
6 cloves
4 peppercorns
1 small stick cinnamon
100 g/4 oz ghee or butter
2 teaspoons sugar
generous litre/2 pints water
salt to taste

Wash and drain the rice. Slice the onions finely. Grind or pound all the spices coarsely. Heat the fat and fry the onions till they are a pale gold. Add the sugar and the spices and fry till the whole is a rich brown. Keep stirring all the time. Add hot water and salt and bring to the boil. Put in the rice and cook till the rice is tender, or turn into an ovenproof dish when the water is nearly gone and put in the oven till the rice is cooked.

This rice is served with a delicious Parsee style curry, Dhansak (see pages 62-3).

TO DRESS UP COLD LEFT-OVER RICE OR FRESHLY BOILED RICE

Oven temperature: Very cool
120°C, 250°F, Gas Mark ½

METRIC/IMPERIAL

50 g/2 oz ghee
¼ teaspoon onion seed
1 teaspoon turmeric
450 g/1 lb cooked rice
salt to taste

In a large pan, heat the ghee and fry the onion seed for 1 minute. Add the turmeric, then the rice and salt. Mix with a fork so that the rice is well coated with the turmeric and ghee. Cover the pan and put in the oven for 10 minutes to heat right through. This is a quick way to dress up rice when unexpected guests arrive.

TOMATO RICE

Oven temperature: Cool
150°C, 300°F, Gas Mark 2

METRIC/IMPERIAL

225 g/8 oz rice
2 onions
1 clove garlic
¼ teaspoon ginger powder
¼ teaspoon chilli powder
50 g/2 oz cooking fat or ghee
¼ teaspoon garam masala
600 ml/1 pint tomato juice
1 teaspoon salt

Wash the rice and soak in cold water for 1 hour. Slice the onions finely. Grind the garlic to a paste and mix in the ginger and chilli.

Heat the fat in a saucepan and fry the onions a golden brown. Add the garlic paste and garam masala and fry till the masala is cooked. Put in the rice and fry till the rice is lightly coloured. Add the tomato juice, salt and sufficient water to come about 2.5 cm/1 inch above the rice. Bring to the boil and cook over low heat till rice is ready, or put into the oven. When the liquid is nearly dry cover and leave till rice is cooked.

KHITCHREE OR KEDGEREE

METRIC/IMPERIAL

100 g/4 oz lentils (masur or mung)
225 g/8 oz rice
1 onion
50 g/2 oz ghee or butter
1 teaspoon cummin seeds
1 small stick cinnamon
4 cloves
1 large cardamom, peeled
½ teaspoon turmeric
salt to taste

Soak lentils for 30 minutes. Wash rice and drain. Slice onion finely. Heat the fat, fry the onions till golden brown and remove. Reserve for garnish. To the hot fat add the washed and drained lentils, cummin seeds, cinnamon, cloves, cardamom and turmeric and fry for 5 minutes, stirring all the time. Add the rice and keep stirring till the rice begins to stick to the pan. Now add hot water and salt. The water should stand 2.5 cm/1 inch above the level of the rice. Bring to the boil then simmer on a very low heat till both the rice and lentils are cooked. Serve garnished with the fried onions.

MASALA KEDGEREE

Oven temperature: Moderately hot
190°C, 375°F, Gas Mark 5

METRIC/IMPERIAL

225 g/8 oz rice
4 oz arhar dal
2 onions
1 clove garlic
¼ teaspoon ginger powder
¼ teaspoon chilli powder
65 g/2½ oz ghee or cooking fat
¼ teaspoon ground cinnamon
½ teaspoon ground cloves
600 ml/1 pint water
2 teaspoons salt
½ teaspoon turmeric

Wash and dry the rice and dal. Roast them in the oven for 10 minutes. Slice the onions finely. Pound the garlic and add to it the ginger and chilli.

Heat the ghee and fry the onions until crisp and brown. Remove half and reserve. Add to the fat and onions the garlic mixture, cinnamon and clove. Stir, add the rice and dal and fry for 5 minutes. Now add hot water, salt and turmeric and simmer till rice and dal are cooked. Add a little more water if required. Serve with fried onions sprinkled on top.

SOFT KEDGEREE

Oven temperature: Moderate
160°C, 325°F, Gas Mark 3

METRIC/IMPERIAL

225 g/8 oz rice
100 g/4 oz masoor dal
¾ teaspoon cummin seeds
5-cm/2-inch stick cinnamon
6-cm/2½-inch piece dry ginger
½ teaspoon turmeric
10 cloves
1 teaspoon salt
100 g/4 oz onions, sliced
4 cloves garlic
10 cardamoms
100 g/4 oz butter

Wash the rice and dal. Put them in a large saucepan with sufficient water to cover them well. Put in all the spices, salt, sliced onions and the peeled garlic and bruised cardamoms. Leave to soak for 3 hours or more. Then cook all together over a medium heat with the butter till rice and dal are tender and the liquid is almost gone. Finish off in the oven for 15 minutes. Serve hot, garnished with fried onions.

SAFFRON KEDGEREE

METRIC/IMPERIAL

15 g/½ oz almonds
15 g/½ oz currants
4 onions
100 g/4 oz freshly grated coconut or 50 g/2 oz desiccated coconut
300 ml/½ pint water
4 threads saffron
½ teaspoon cummin seeds
10 cardamoms
½ teaspoon ginger powder or two 2.5-cm/1-inch pieces green ginger
175 g/6 oz cooking fat or oil
225 g/8 oz rice
100 g/4 oz tuar or arhar dal
200 ml/7 fl oz water
2½ teaspoons salt
8 green chillies
10 cloves
4 small sticks cinnamon
50 g/2 oz sugar

Blanch and slice the almonds. Wash and dry the currants. Slice the onions thinly. Soak the coconut in hot water for 10 minutes, then squeeze out the milk and strain. Dry roast the saffron and mix in the coconut milk. Coarsely grind the cummin and cardamom seeds. If green ginger is used, scrape and slice very thinly. Heat the fat and fry the almonds and currants till the almonds are medium brown. Remove and reserve. Fry the onions till they are crisp and brown. Wash the rice and the dal. In one saucepan put in 150 ml/¼ pint water, the rice and 1 teaspoon salt. Half cook the rice and put into a large pan. In another pan put the remaining water, the dal and 1 teaspoon salt and cook till half done. Add this to the rice. Add also another ½ teaspoon salt, the saffron mixed with coconut milk, most of the almonds and currants, fried onions, green chillies (sliced), sliced ginger and the other spices. Add the sugar and the fat in which the onions were fried. Mix thoroughly and cover with a lid. Bring to the boil and simmer till rice and dal are cooked. Mix the kedgeree with a fork and leave on a very low heat for 5 minutes more. Remove and serve sprinkled with the remaining almonds and currants.

FISH KEDGEREE

METRIC/IMPERIAL

1 plaice or 18 prawns
1 tablespoon salt
4 green chillies
½ bunch coriander or watercress leaves
4 onions
225 g/8 oz freshly grated or 100 g/4 oz desiccated coconut
225 g/8 oz rice
100 g/4 oz tuar dal
40 g/1½ oz melted butter or cooking fat
1 teaspoon ginger powder
2 sticks cinnamon
5 cloves
½ teaspoon cummin seeds
1 teaspoon turmeric

If plaice is used, cut the fish into 1-cm/½-inch pieces. Wash and marinate the pieces in ½ tablespoon salt and leave for 30 minutes. If fresh prawns are used, remove the shells and the black thread at the back, then wash and salt and leave for 30 minutes. If boiled prawns are used do not salt them. Chop the chillies and the green leaves. Slice the onions finely. Soak the coconut in 600 ml/1 pint of hot water and leave for 10 minutes, then squeeze and strain. Reserve the milk. Wash the rice and dal separately. Put the dal in a pan with 600 ml/1 pint of water and boil till soft. Remove from heat. In another saucepan, fry 1 sliced onion in 15 g/½ oz of the fat till cream coloured. Add the chillies and coriander leaves and stir for 3 minutes. Put in the salted fish pieces, or the salted or boiled prawns and ½ tablespoon salt. If plaice or boiled prawns are used add 4 tablespoons of water but if raw prawns are used add 300 ml/½ pint of water. Cook till the fish are half done. Put the rest of the fat in a clean saucepan and fry the rest of the onions until a medium cream colour. Put in the ginger, cinnamon, cloves and the cummin seeds and stir. Add the turmeric, salt and coconut milk and bring to the boil. Add the rice and cooked dal. Simmer till the rice is almost cooked and add the fish. If plaice is used the rice should be quite cooked but if prawns are used the rice should be undercooked. Simmer till the rice is soft and there is no more liquid left. Serve hot.

VEGETABLE KEDGEREE

METRIC/IMPERIAL

- 350 g/12 oz freshly grated or 175 g/6 oz desiccated coconut
- 1 cucumber
- 175 g/6 oz tomatoes
- 175 g/6 oz potatoes
- 175 g/6 oz carrots
- 3 green bananas
- 4 onions
- 3 cloves garlic
- coriander or watercress
- 5 green chillies or ¼ green pepper
- 2 tablespoons desiccated coconut
- 50 g/2 oz melted butter or cooking oil
- 3 teaspoons salt
- 3 tablespoons tuar dal
- 3 tablespoons chana dal
- 3 tablespoons mung dal
- 3 tablespoons masoor dal
- ¾ teaspoon cummin powder
- 1 teaspoon garam masala
- ½ teaspoon ginger powder
- 1 teaspoon turmeric
- 225g/8 oz rice

Soak the fresh or desiccated coconut in 900 ml/1½ pints of hot water and leave for 10 minutes. Squeeze out the milk, strain and reserve the milk. Peel and dice all the vegetables and fruit in large cubes. Slice the onions finely and divide into two portions. Chop the garlic and few green coriander leaves. Slice the chillies. Soak the 2 tablespoons desiccated coconut in ½ tablespoon hot water. Fry the vegetables separately in half the oil till they are half cooked. Put 1 teaspoon salt in 1 tablespoon water and, as the vegetables are removed from the pan, sprinkle them with the salt water. Keep the fried vegetables warm. Wash all the dals separately. Put the tuar dal in a generous litre/2 pints water; cook till the grains are soft. Add to it the chana dal and when the chana grains are soft remove from the heat and mix in the other two dals, mung and masoor. Set aside. Fry half the onions to a cream colour in the rest of the oil and remove. In the same fat fry the cummin powder, then the garam masala, then the ginger, garlic, coriander leaves and soaked coconut for 5 minutes. Add the turmeric and remaining salt and fry for another 5 minutes, stirring all the time. Add the fried onions, the dals and the rice (washed and drained). Add the 900 ml/1½ pints coconut milk, the raw sliced onions and all the fried vegetables. Simmer; if rice is not cooked after 20 minutes and the liquid is dry, add 300 ml/½ pint hot water and simmer till the rice is tender.

CHICKEN PULAO

Oven temperature: Moderate
160°C, 325°F, Gas Mark 3

METRIC/IMPERIAL

450 g/1 lb rice
2 large onions, sliced
2 teaspoons poppy seeds
8 cloves
8 green cardamoms
150 ml/¼ pint yogurt
2 teaspoons coriander powder
1 teaspoon ginger powder
1 (1-kg/2-lb) chicken
225 g/8 oz ghee or butter
2 medium onions, sliced finely
1.75 litres/3 pints water
salt
150 ml/¼ pint milk
few strands saffron

Wash rice and soak in water for 30 minutes. Grind the 2 sliced onions, poppy seeds, 4 cloves and 4 cardamoms. Put the yogurt in a bowl; add the ground spices, the coriander and ginger powders. Mix well and rub the trussed chicken inside as well as outside with the yogurt mixture. Leave the bird in the yogurt.

In a large pan heat the ghee and fry the sliced onions golden brown, add the chicken and the yogurt and fry. When fried on all sides cover and simmer gently till the chicken is tender.

Boil the rice in the water with salt, 4 cardamoms and 4

cloves. When the rice is cooked, drain. Cover the chicken with the rice, sprinkle with milk and saffron and put in the oven for 10 minutes. It is better to drain the rice before it is completely cooked so that there is no possibility of the rice becoming mushy.

PULAO
(Meat or chicken)

METRIC/IMPERIAL

350 g/12 oz rice
450 g/1 lb meat or chicken
1 teaspoon saffron threads
2 tablespoons lemon juice
4 medium onions
2 cloves garlic
½ teaspoon ginger powder
1 tablespoon garam masala
600 ml/1 pint yogurt
1 tablespoon salt
2 tablespoons sugar
40 g/1½ oz melted butter

Wash and drain the rice. Wash the meat or chicken and cut into large pieces.

Dry fry the saffron, crumble and put into the lemon juice. Slice the onions and grind the garlic. Make a paste of the garlic and ginger. Fry one onion golden brown and remove. Rub the garlic paste into the meat or chicken and put into a bowl with ¾ tablespoon garam masala, half of the saffron juice, 450 ml/¾ pint yogurt, fried onion and half the salt. Mix all together and leave for 1 hour.

Turn the contents of the bowl into a saucepan and simmer over a very low heat till the meat is tender.

Take a large saucepan and fill it three-quarters full of water. Bring to the boil and add the rice. Cook on brisk heat till the rice is nearly ready, drain and put the rice into a bowl with the rest of the yogurt, garam masala, sliced onions, sugar, melted butter and the rest of the salt. Mix thoroughly. Now put half the rice mixture in a saucepan, then the meat and gravy, the remaining saffron juice and the rest of the rice. Cover and simmer over low heat till the rice is cooked. Stir with a fork occasionally.

MEAT PULAO

Oven temperature: Moderate
160°C, 325°F, Gas Mark 3

METRIC/IMPERIAL

3 cloves garlic
4 green chillies
½ bunch coriander or watercress leaves
450 g/1 lb lean minced meat
1 potato
½ teaspoon ginger powder
½ green pepper, chopped
½ teaspoon turmeric
4 teaspoons salt
450 g/1 lb onions
50 g/2 oz almonds
100 g/4 oz currants
pinch of saffron
juice of 2 lemons
175 g/6 oz sugar
1 kg/2 lb meat
350 g/12 oz melted butter
100 g/4 oz desiccated coconut
450 g/1 lb rice
½ teaspoon grated nutmeg
½ teaspoon mace powder
425 g/15 oz yogurt
1 teaspoon cummin seeds
½ teaspoon black pepper

Chop the garlic, green chillies and coriander leaves and mix with the minced meat. Peel, boil and mash the potato and add to the mince. Add also the ginger, green pepper, turmeric and a teaspoon of salt. Mix thoroughly and leave for an hour or more.

Slice all the onions finely. Blanch the almonds and slice them. Clean and wash the currants and mix with almonds. Dry roast the saffron and crumble into the juice of the lemons. Boil the sugar in 300 ml/½ pint of water.

Wash and cut the meat into large pieces. Melt 25 g/1 oz of the butter in saucepan and fry 1 sliced onion with 1 teaspoon salt. When the onion is dark brown, put in the meat and stir till the meat is well browned. Now add 1.75 litres/3 pints of water and bring to the boil, then simmer slowly till the meat is cooked and only 300 ml/½ pint of water remains.

Now make the mince into little balls the size of large marbles. Fry them in 225 g/8 oz butter and set aside. Fry the currants and almonds in 40 g/1½ oz melted butter, drain and set aside. In the same fat fry all the sliced onions except one, till crisp. Soak the coconut in 450 ml/¾ boiling water, cover and leave for 10 minutes. Squeeze and strain out the milk.

Wash the rice and divide into two portions. In a saucepan, bring 450 ml/¾ pint water to the boil. Add 1 teaspoon salt and half the rice. Cook till rice is half done. Add the lemon juice and saffron and mix well. Remove from heat but keep warm. In another pan, heat 40 g/1½ oz butter, 1 teaspoon salt, the reserved sliced onion and the coconut milk. Bring to the boil and add the other 225 g/8 oz rice. Cook till half done and remove from heat. Take a large bowl and put in the plain white rice which you have just cooked, with onion, the meat and gravy, almonds, currants, fried onions, nutmeg, mace, meat balls and the fat in which they were cooked. Add also the yogurt, cummin seeds and half the sugar syrup. Mix thoroughly and divide into three portions. Pour the other half of the syrup over the saffron rice and divide it into two portions. Take a large pan with tight-fitting lid. Spread part of the white rice at the bottom then part of the saffron rice and so on. Season with black pepper. Put the lid on tightly and bake in a moderate oven for 25 minutes. Turn upside down on to a hot serving dish carefully so that the layers remain intact.

MEAT OR CHICKEN YAKHNI PULAO

Oven temperature: Moderate
160°C, 325°F, Gas Mark 3

METRIC/IMPERIAL

1 kg/2 lb meat or chicken
2 large onions, sliced finely
2 bay leaves
4 peppercorns
4 cloves
1 stick cinnamon
salt to taste
100 g/4 oz ghee or butter
450 g/1 lb rice
50 g/2 oz raisins
pinch of saffron (optional)
1 teaspoon milk
50 g/2 oz almonds

Cut the meat into 5-cm/2-inch pieces, or if chicken is used cut into joints. Put half the sliced onions, the meat and spices tied in muslin (bay leaves, peppercorns, cloves and cinnamon) in a saucepan with 1.75 litres/3 pints water and bring to the boil. Simmer gently till the meat is tender. Add salt to taste. Remove the meat from the liquid and keep aside. Strain the liquid and add water if necessary to make up to a generous litre/2 pints.

In a large saucepan heat the ghee and fry the rest of the sliced onions a golden brown. Take the onions out and keep aside. Put the meat in the hot fat and fry gently till the meat is dry. Remove meat to a platter.

In the same fat fry the rice for 5 minutes, add the raisins and fry for another minute. Now add the generous litre/2 pints stock and bring to the boil. Simmer, covered, till water is absorbed.

Turn into an ovenproof dish, add the meat and saffron soaked in milk, cover, and put in the oven for 20 minutes till rice is cooked. Serve garnished with fried onions and almonds.

KEEMA PULAO

Oven temperature: Moderate
160°C, 325°F, Gas Mark 3

METRIC/IMPERIAL

100 g/4 oz onions, finely sliced
225 g/8 oz ghee or butter
450 g/1 lb lean minced meat
2 teaspoons coriander powder
1 teaspoon ginger powder
1 teaspoon chilli powder
2 tablespoons yogurt
a few strands saffron
salt to taste
450 g/1 lb rice
8 cloves
1 stick cinnamon

Fry the onions in the fat till golden brown. Add the mince and all the spices except the cloves and cinnamon. Cook till the mince is lightly browned then add the yogurt and fry till the mince is a rich brown. Soak the saffron in water and add to the mince. Add salt, stir and remove from the heat.

Wash and drain the rice. Put the rice, cloves, cinnamon and 2 teaspoons salt in a large pan. Add enough water to come 5 cm/2 inches above the level of the rice. Bring to the boil, cover and simmer till the water is almost dry and the rice nearly cooked. Remove from the heat.

Take a large casserole and put in a layer of rice then a layer of mince and so on till all the mince and rice are used up. The last layer must be rice. Put on the lid and place in the oven for 20 minutes till the rice is cooked. Before serving mix the pulao very carefully so as not to break the rice grains.

PRAWN OR SHRIMP PULAO

Oven temperature: Moderate
160°C, 325°F, Gas Mark 3

METRIC/IMPERIAL

175 g/6 oz tomatoes
100 g/4 oz ghee or butter
2 teaspoons garam masala
1 teaspoon chilli powder
½ teaspoon ginger powder
salt to taste
450 g/1 lb prawns or shrimps
225 g/8 oz rice
2 green cardamoms
4 cloves
4 peppercorns
small stick cinnamon

Chop the tomatoes. Heat the ghee in a saucepan. Add the tomatoes, garam masala, chilli, ginger and salt and cook for 5 minutes, stirring all the time. Now add prawns and cook over a low heat in a covered pan till the prawns are tender.

Boil 1.75 litres/3 pints water in another pan, and add the washed and drained rice, with the cardamoms, cloves, peppercorns and cinnamon tied in muslin. Boil uncovered till the rice is cooked and drain in a colander. In an ovenproof dish put a layer of rice, then a layer of the curry, then a layer of rice. Cover and put in the oven for 10 minutes.

KEEMA-MATAR PULAO
(Minced Meat and Pea)

Oven temperature: Moderate
160°C, 325°F, Gas Mark 3

METRIC/IMPERIAL

450 g/1 lb rice
1 medium onion
1 clove garlic
½ teaspoon ginger powder
100 g/4 oz ghee or butter
1 teaspoon cummin seeds
4 cloves
225 g/8 oz minced meat
4 tablespoons yogurt
450 g/1 lb shelled peas
salt to taste
2 teaspoons garam masala

Wash and soak the rice for 30 minutes. Grind the onion and garlic and mix in the ginger powder. In a large pan heat the ghee and add the cummin seeds and the cloves. When the cloves swell and come to the surface add the ground onion paste and fry over a low heat.

Now add the minced meat and fry for a few minutes, then add the yogurt and fry till a rich brown. Add the peas and simmer till done. Add a little water if required. Drain the rice and add to the mince with salt and enough hot water to come 2.5 cm/1 inch above the rice. Bring to the boil and simmer covered till the water is nearly evaporated.

Put into the oven after sprinkling with garam masala. Cover and cook for 20 minutes.

VEGETABLE PULAO

Oven temperature: Moderate
160°C, 325°F, Gas Mark 3

METRIC/IMPERIAL

225 g/8 oz rice
2 medium onions
175 g/6 oz ghee or butter
50 g/2 oz cauliflower
50 g/2 oz potatoes, diced
50 g/2 oz shelled peas
50 g/2 oz carrots, sliced
50 g/2 oz French beans, sliced
½ teaspoon ginger powder
2 cardamoms, peeled
1 bay leaf
4 cloves
4 peppercorns
½ teaspoon turmeric
salt to taste

Wash rice and drain. Slice onions finely. Heat the fat in a large saucepan and fry the onions golden brown. Remove and keep warm.

Fry the other vegetables in the fat, one kind at a time, and keep aside. Now add the spices and fry till the cloves rise to the surface. Add the rice and fry for 2 minutes, stirring all the time. Add 900 ml/1½ pints boiling water and salt and boil till the water is nearly all evaporated. Turn into an ovenproof dish, add the fried vegetables, cover and put in the oven for 15-20 minutes. Serve with the fried onions sprinkled on top.

MOTI PULAO

Oven temperature: Moderate
160°C, 325°F, Gas Mark 3

METRIC/IMPERIAL

450 g/1 lb lean meat, minced very finely
2 teaspoons coriander powder
2 teaspoons garam masala
salt to taste
6 tablespoons yogurt
225 g/8 oz ghee or butter
1 teaspoon ginger powder
4 green chillies
450 g/1 lb rice
100 g/4 oz raisins
100 g/4 oz almonds, blanched

Put the mince in a bowl and add the coriander powder, 1 teaspoon garam masala, salt, 2 tablespoons yogurt and 50 g/2 oz ghee. Mix thoroughly and make into very small balls.

Put the rest of the ghee in a large saucepan and fry the rest of the yogurt and the garam masala till they are a rich brown. Add the ginger powder, stir, then add the meat balls. Fry gently till the balls are cooked. Add the chopped green chillies and 300 ml/½ pint hot water. Simmer, covered, for 10 minutes. Take the meat balls out of the pan and keep aside. Leave the fat in the pan for later use.

Boil 3.5 litres/6 pints water in a large pan. Add the rice and salt and cook till the rice is ready. Drain the rice in a colander and put it in the fat in the pan in which the meat balls were cooked.

In a frying pan fry the raisins and the blanched almonds and add these to the rice. Put the rice in the oven for 10 minutes. Before serving, mix the rice and put on a flat dish. Scatter the meat balls on top.

PEA PULAO

Oven temperature: Moderate
160°C, 325°F, Gas Mark 3

METRIC/IMPERIAL

100 g/4 oz ghee or butter
450 g/1 lb rice
225-275 g/8-10 oz green peas
2 teaspoons salt
600 ml/1 pint water

Heat the fat and add the washed and drained rice. Fry for 5 minutes then add the peas and salt. Keep stirring all the time as the rice is liable to stick. After 2–3 minutes add the water and bring to the boil. Simmer gently till the water is nearly absorbed. Turn into an ovenproof dish. Cover and put in the oven for about 20 minutes until the rice is cooked.

STUFFED PEPPER PULAO

Oven temperature: Moderate
160°C, 325°F, Gas Mark 3

METRIC/IMPERIAL

4 medium green peppers
75 g/3 oz ghee
1 onion, sliced finely
½ teaspoon turmeric
½ teaspoon onion seeds
450 g/1 lb rice
salt to taste

for stuffing:

225 g/8 oz potatoes
1 onion
50 g/2 oz ghee or butter
225 g/8 oz shelled peas
½ teaspoon turmeric
¼ teaspoon ginger powder
salt to taste
½ teaspoon chilli powder or 2 green chillies, chopped
½ teaspoon garam masala

To make the stuffing, boil, peel and dice potatoes. Chop the onion. Heat the fat and fry the onion for 3 minutes. Add the peas, potatoes, turmeric, ginger and salt and fry for another 3 minutes. Cover and cook over low heat till the peas are cooked. Add the chilli powder or the green chillies and the garam masala and remove from the heat. Cut off the tops of the peppers and stuff them with the vegetables. Cover with the tops and secure them with wooden cocktail sticks.

In another pan heat the 75 g/3 oz ghee and fry the onion. When the onion is lightly browned add the turmeric, onion seeds, rice and salt and fry for 3–4 minutes. Add sufficient hot water to stand 2.5 cm/1 inch above the level of the rice. Boil and when the water is nearly dry turn into an ovenproof dish. Put the peppers on the rice, cover dish and put in the oven for 20 minutes or more till the rice is cooked.

DRIED FRUIT PULAO

Oven temperature: Moderate
160°C, 325°F, Gas Mark 3

METRIC/IMPERIAL

1 kg/2 lb meat
225 g/8 oz onions
15 almonds
9 pistachios or walnuts
350 g/12 oz rice
1 tablespoon salt
225 g/8 oz ghee or cooking fat
1 teaspoon ginger powder
2 teaspoons coriander powder
2 tablespoons garam masala
½ teaspoon cummin powder
5 eggs
225 g/8 oz minced meat
12 dried apricots
9 currants
4 teaspoons sugar

Wash and cut meat into large cubes. Slice the onions finely. Blanch and slice the almonds. Shell the pistachios or walnuts. Wash and drain the rice. Parboil the rice with ½ tablespoon salt. Drain. Heat half the ghee and fry the onions until golden brown. Add ginger, fry for 1 minute, then add the meat and the rest of the salt, coriander and 900 ml/1½ pints warm water. Simmer till meat is tender. Remove from heat and take out the meat. There should be about 600 ml/1 pint of gravy left. Add the rice to the gravy. Simmer and cook till rice is soft. Fork the rice occasionally so that it does not burn.

In another saucepan put 50 g/2 oz ghee. Heat and add 1 tablespoon garam masala, the cooked meat and cummin. Put over this a layer of rice, cover, and place in the oven for 30 minutes.

Take another saucepan and put in the rest of the ghee. Separate the eggs and fry the yolks one at a time. Remove the fried yolks and reserve. In the same fat fry the mince till reddish brown. Add a little water and remaining garam masala, the dried fruits, nuts and egg whites and cook for 10 minutes. When the liquid is absorbed put mixture over the rice. Cover with remaining rice, yolks and sugar. Simmer over low heat for 5 minutes and serve.

FISH PULAO

Oven temperature: Moderate
160°C, 325°F, Gas Mark 3

METRIC/IMPERIAL

1 kg/2 lb fish cutlets (firm-fleshed fish should be used)	salt to taste
2 large onions	450 g/1 lb rice
175 g/6 oz ghee or butter	1 stick cinnamon
2 teaspoons coriander powder	1 large peeled cardamom
2 teaspoons chilli powder	6 cloves
	2 teaspoons garam masala

Wash and drain the fish. Slice onions finely and fry them in the ghee till golden brown. Lower heat and fry the coriander, chilli and fish. When the fish is brown remove from the heat and keep aside.

Boil 3.5 litres/6 pints water and add salt, the washed and drained rice, and cinnamon, cardamom and cloves tied in muslin. When the rice is cooked, drain in a colander. In a casserole, put a layer of rice, then a layer of fish curry and so on ending with a layer of rice. Sprinkle garam masala on the top, cover and put in the oven for 15–20 minutes.

MUTTON BIRYANI

Oven temperature: Moderate
160°C, 325°F, Gas Mark 3

METRIC/IMPERIAL

450 g/1 lb mutton
6 peppercorns
4 green cardamoms
2 teaspoons shah zeera (black cummin seeds)
175 g/6 oz ghee
225 g/8 oz onions, sliced finely
4 tablespoons yogurt
salt to taste
2 teaspoons coriander powder
1 teaspoon chilli powder
450 g/1 lb rice
2 bay leaves
50 g/2 oz blanched almonds

Cut the meat into 3.5-cm/1½-inch pieces. Grind the peppercorns, cardamoms and half the cummin seeds. Heat half the ghee and fry the onions till a light brown. Take out half the onions and keep aside.

Put the meat, yogurt and salt into the pan with the remaining onions and simmer till the meat is cooked and is a rich brown. Stir occasionally while cooking. Add the ground spices, coriander and chilli and fry over a low heat for a few minutes till well mixed.

Take a large pan which can fit into the oven and heat the rest of the ghee in it. Add the washed and drained rice and bay leaves and fry for 4 minutes. Add the remaining cummin seeds, onions and salt and continue frying. Take out nearly all the rice, leaving a layer at the bottom of the pan. Put a layer of meat on this, then a layer of rice and so on, ending with a top layer of rice. Garnish with blanched almonds. Add enough water to come 2.5 cm/1 inch above the level of the rice. Put on the heat and bring to the boil; simmer till the water has evaporated. Put in the oven for 20 minutes.

KUTCHI BIRYANI OR RAW PULAO

Oven temperature: Moderate
160°C, 325°F, Gas Mark 3

METRIC/IMPERIAL

675 g/1½ lb rice
2 large onions
1 kg/2 lb meat or chicken
pinch saffron strands
3 tablespoons mixed milk and water
300 ml/½ pint yogurt
salt to taste
100 g/4 oz ghee or butter
1 teaspoon ginger powder
4 cardamoms
1 teaspoon shah zeera (black cummin seeds)
4 cloves
1 stick cinnamon
4 green chillies
few sprigs of mint
2 cloves garlic

Wash the rice and soak in cold water for 30 minutes. Slice the onions finely. Cut the meat or chicken into pieces. Soak the saffron in the milk and water. Put the yogurt in a bowl, add to it the meat and salt and leave for 15 minutes.

Take a large pan which will fit into the oven and heat the ghee in it; fry the sliced onions a golden brown. Add the meat and yogurt and the dry spices and cook for 15 minutes, stirring often. Add the whole green chillies and mint sprigs. Drain the rice and put on top of the meat.

Grind the garlic and mix with 600 ml/1 pint water. Sprinkle this garlic water on the rice. Pour the saffron water and the strands on top also. Cover and bring to the boil, then put in the oven for 45 minutes or more till the rice is cooked.

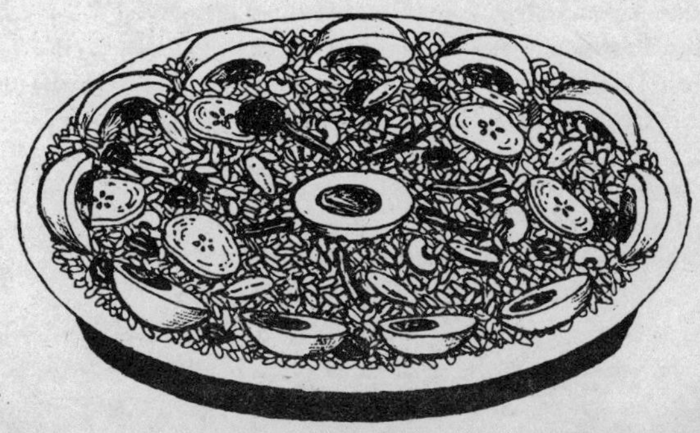

CHICKEN OR LAMB BIRYANI

Oven temperature: Moderate
180°C, 350°F, Gas Mark 4 160°C, 325°F, Gas Mark 3

METRIC/IMPERIAL

for meat:

1.25 kg/2½ lb lamb or chicken
1 teaspoon coriander powder
½ teaspoon ground cloves
1 teaspoon cummin powder
¼ teaspoon black pepper
1 teaspoon chilli powder
½ teaspoon ground cinnamon
½ teaspoon cardamom powder
300 ml/½ pint yogurt
juice of 1 lemon
3 cloves garlic
salt to taste
2.5-cm/1-inch piece fresh ginger or 1 teaspoon ginger powder
4 large onions
225 g/8 oz ghee or butter

for rice:

675 g/1½ lb rice
5 bay leaves
6 green cardamoms
10 cloves
4 small sticks cinnamon
10 peppercorns
4 teaspoons salt
½ teaspoon saffron strands
2 teaspoons milk

Wash meat, cut into pieces and put into a bowl with the ground spices, yogurt, lemon juice, finely chopped garlic and salt. If fresh ginger is used, chop finely and add to meat. Slice the onions finely and fry in the ghee till crisp and golden brown. Remove and put two-thirds into the meat mixture.

Soak the rice for 1 hour before cooking. Take a large pan and fill three-quarters full with water. Put in the spices and salt and bring to the boil. Add the rice and remove from the heat after 6 minutes. Drain thoroughly, then spread out on a flat dish to cool.

Mix the saffron in the hot milk. In a large pan, put in the meat and yogurt mixture and cover with the rice; pour over the ghee in which the onions were fried and the saffron and milk.

Bring to the boil, then put in the oven for 1 hour or more. After 30 minutes reduce heat. Mix before serving with fried onions sprinkled on top.

Meat

Because of religious taboos in relation to meat, sheep and goats provide most of the meat that is commonly eaten in India. Venison is considered a delicacy.

The most elaborate forms of cooking meat are to be found in the north, and in the areas where Mogul influence predominated. The simpler preparations introduced by the Moguls from central Asia became more and more elaborate in response to economic and cultural development and greater sophistication in the way of life.

For example, the simple grilled kabab developed into scores of different varieties, so much so that in some places it became customary for cooks, called kababchis, to specialize in just that one particular dish.

MEAT OR CHICKEN CURRY

METRIC/IMPERIAL

1 kg/2 lb lean meat or 1 (1.25-kg/2½-lb) chicken
450 g/1 lb onions
4 cloves garlic
2 teaspoons water
1 teaspoon turmeric
1 teaspoon cummin powder
2 teaspoons coriander powder
1 teaspoon ginger powder
2 teaspoons chilli powder
1 teaspoon paprika
2 teaspoons poppy seeds (optional)
100 g/4 oz ghee or other cooking medium
salt to taste
2 bay leaves
150 ml/¼ pint yogurt or 225 g/8 oz tomatoes
1 teaspoon garam masala

Wash, dry and cut meat into 2.5-cm/1-inch cubes or joint the chicken. Slice half the onions finely. Grind the rest of the onions and garlic to a paste. Add water to the paste and mix in the turmeric, cummin, coriander, ginger and chilli powders and paprika. If poppy seeds are used, they should be ground and added to the paste.

Heat the ghee and fry the sliced onions until golden brown. Lower heat, add the paste and fry for 3–4 minutes, stirring all the time. Add the meat and salt and increase the heat. Fry for 5 minutes.

Add the bay leaves and yogurt or tomatoes (quartered), mix thoroughly, cover and simmer till the meat is almost tender. Add garam masala and fry for 2–3 minutes. Cover and simmer till cooked through.

If the liquid dries up while cooking, add hot water, 2 tablespoons at a time. Stir often so that the curry does not stick to the pan. Serve with rice or bread.

BEEF OR MUTTON CHILLI CURRY

METRIC/IMPERIAL

1 walnut-size lump of tamarind pulp
450 g/1 lb lean meat
2 medium onions
2 cloves garlic
2–3 green chillies
50 g/2 oz ghee or oil
1 teaspoon cummin powder
1 teaspoon turmeric
2 teaspoons chilli powder
1 teaspoon ginger powder
salt to taste

Soak the tamarind in 2 tablespoons water. Cut the meat into 2.5-cm/1-inch cubes. Slice the onions finely and chop the garlic. Chop the green chillies.

Heat the ghee and fry the onions and garlic till lightly browned. Lower heat and add the spices and green chillies and cook, covered, for 5 minutes.

Add the meat and salt and stir thoroughly, then cover and cook for 10 minutes.

Add 150 ml/¼ pint warm water and simmer till the meat is tender. Squeeze the tamarind and strain the juice. Add this juice to the curry and fry for 5–6 minutes till the gravy is thick.

This is a very hot curry and is served with plain boiled rice.

PARSEE MUTTON CURRY

METRIC/IMPERIAL

450 g/1 lb mutton
450 g/1 lb potatoes
2 cloves garlic
100 g/4 oz ground almonds
1 tablespoon ground peanuts
½ teaspoon chilli powder
1 tablespoon coriander powder
¼ teaspoon cummin powder
½ teaspoon turmeric
1 teaspoon ginger powder
1 tablespoon besan
225 g/8 oz cooking fat
½ green pepper, chopped
300 ml/½ pint coconut milk
150 ml/¼ pint tamarind water
salt to taste

Cut mutton and potatoes in cubes. Chop garlic very fine. Mix ground almonds, peanuts, chilli, coriander, cummin, turmeric, ginger and besan. Boil the mutton in water to cover until soft.

In another saucepan heat the fat and fry the mixed spices for at least 5–7 minutes. Add the meat, stock and potatoes. When the potatoes are soft add the chopped pepper, coconut milk and tamarind water. Season with salt.

Simmer until the gravy thickens. When fat floats on top remove from heat. Skim before serving if wished.

MUTTON AND PEA CURRY

METRIC/IMPERIAL

100 g/4 oz dried peas
450 g/1 lb meat
3 potatoes, peeled and cubed
50 g/2 oz cooking fat
1 teaspoon garam masala
1 onion, sliced
1 clove garlic, sliced
½ teaspoon ginger powder
¼ teaspoon chilli powder
½ teaspoon coriander powder
½ teaspoon turmeric
½ teaspoon cummin powder
¼ green pepper, chopped
½ teaspoon sugar
1 teaspoon salt
1 teaspoon cornflour mixed with 1 tablespoon water

Soak peas overnight. Clean and cut meat into cubes. Fry the potatoes lightly in the heated fat.

Add the garam masala, onion and garlic and fry for another 5 minutes. Add the drained peas and powdered ginger, chilli, coriander, turmeric and cummin and fry for 5 minutes, then pour in 600 ml/1 pint hot water and simmer till meat is nearly tender.

Put in the potatoes, chopped green pepper, sugar and salt. Cook till meat is quite soft and done.

Remove the meat and potatoes, add the cornflour paste to the gravy and thicken. Put in the meat and potatoes and stir.

Serve hot.

STEWING STEAK CURRY

METRIC/IMPERIAL

450 g/1 lb stewing steak
75 g/3 oz desiccated coconut
300 ml/½ pint hot water
2 tablespoons coriander seeds
1 large onion
½ teaspoon garlic salt, or 5 cloves garlic
4 tablespoons hot milk
4 large potatoes
50 g/2 oz cooking fat
1 teaspoon turmeric
¼ teaspoon chilli powder
½ teaspoon ginger powder
½ teaspoon cummin powder
2 teaspoons salt
juice of ½ lemon

Cut the meat into cubes. Soak 50 g/2 oz coconut in the hot water for 10 minutes. Squeeze and strain out the milk.

In a dry frying pan roast the coriander seeds lightly then grind them. Slice the onion finely. If fresh garlic is used, grind. Soak 25 g/1 oz coconut in the hot milk. Peel and quarter the potatoes.

Heat the fat, brown the onion and add all the ground spices; cook for 3 minutes. Then add the coconut and milk mixture, meat and salt and simmer for 5 minutes. Add the strained coconut milk and bring to the boil. Add the potatoes and simmer till both meat and potatoes are tender. Add lemon juice.

If more gravy is required add a little hot water to thin down the liquid.

MEAT AND CABBAGE CURRY

METRIC/IMPERIAL

1 medium cabbage
450 g/1 lb meat
2 teaspoons coriander powder
1 teaspoon turmeric
1 teaspoon ginger powder
¼ teaspoon chilli powder
2 cloves garlic, mashed
150 ml/¼ pint yogurt
225 g/8 oz tomatoes, chopped
2 teaspoons salt
300 ml/½ pint water
2 onions
50 g/2 oz cooking fat
juice of 1 lemon

Cut the cabbage in thin slices and steep in cold, salted water for 30 minutes. Cube the meat and place in a saucepan. Add spices, garlic, yogurt, chopped tomatoes, salt and the water and mix well. Slice the onions thinly and place on top.

Over these place the slices of cabbage, well drained, and then the cooking fat. Bring to the boil then simmer gently until the ingredients are cooked and the liquid is absorbed.

Squeeze in the lemon juice and simmer for about 10 minutes further.

MEAT AND CAULIFLOWER CURRY

METRIC/IMPERIAL

1 kg/2 lb meat
2 cloves garlic
2 onions
1 small cauliflower
salt
100 g/4 oz ghee
1½ teaspoons turmeric
1½ teaspoons cummin powder
1 teaspoon ginger powder
2½ teaspoons coriander powder
2½ teaspoons chilli powder
4 tablespoons yogurt
cooking fat for deep frying
1 teaspoon garam masala

Wash and cut meat into 5-cm/2-inch cubes. Grind the garlic to a paste. Slice the onions finely. Divide the cauliflower into florets, wash and drain. Sprinkle with salt.

Heat the ghee and fry the onions until golden brown. Add all the spices except the garam masala, the yogurt, meat and more salt to taste. Fry for 5 minutes then simmer gently till the meat is cooked. Fry the cauliflower in deep fat till slightly brown. Drain and add to the meat. Stir very carefully so as not to break the cauliflower. Sprinkle with garam masala.

MEAT AND SPINACH CURRY

METRIC/IMPERIAL

1 kg/2 lb lean meat
2 onions
2 cloves garlic
100 g/4 oz ghee
1 teaspoon turmeric
2 teaspoons coriander powder
1 teaspoon ginger powder
2 teaspoons chilli powder
1 teaspoon cummin powder
1 teaspoon garam masala
4 tablespoons yogurt
salt to taste
450 g/1 lb spinach

Cut the meat into 5-cm/2-inch cubes. Slice the onions finely. Crush the garlic. Fry the onions in the hot ghee till golden brown, then add the crushed garlic, the powdered spices and the yogurt. Fry over gentle heat for 3 minutes. Add the meat and salt and fry till the meat is nicely browned. Cover and simmer for 5 minutes.

Pick over and wash the spinach. Chop it finely and add to the meat. Cover and simmer, stirring occasionally, till the meat is tender. Take the lid off and cook till the liquid is absorbed.

MEAT AND POTATO CURRY

METRIC/IMPERIAL

450 g/1 lb beef or mutton
4–5 potatoes
1 large onion
3 cloves garlic
50 g/2 oz cooking fat
1 teaspoon ginger powder
1 teaspoon turmeric
2 teaspoons coriander powder
2 teaspoons garam masala
½ teaspoon chilli powder
2–2½ teaspoons salt
150 ml/¼ pint yogurt
3 tomatoes, sliced thinly
450 ml/¾ pint water
juice of ½ lemon

Cut the meat in small pieces. Cube the potatoes. Cut the onion in thin slices and mash the cloves of garlic. Fry the onion in melted fat until golden brown. Add the ginger, garlic, turmeric, coriander, garam masala, chilli and salt and fry together for 3–4 minutes. Add yogurt and thinly sliced tomatoes and let the mixture cook for 5 minutes on medium heat.

Add the meat and stir well, letting it cook another 5 minutes. Add 300 ml/½ pint of the water, cover the saucepan and let the meat cook for about 30 minutes (until it is half cooked).

Add the potatoes and mix well. Pour in the rest of the water. Cook until meat and potatoes are done, about 30 minutes more. Add lemon juice and simmer gently for 5 minutes.

If more gravy is required, more hot water can be added, up to 150 ml/¼ pint in quantity.

HUSSAINY CURRY (1)

METRIC/IMPERIAL

450 g/1 lb cold mutton, beef or lamb
2.5-cm/1-inch piece fresh ginger
2 medium onions
2 teaspoons poppy seeds
2 cloves garlic
1 tablespoon desiccated or 2 tablespoons fresh coconut
100 g/4 oz ghee
2 teaspoons coriander powder
pinch of clove powder
1 teaspoon turmeric
1 teaspoon chilli powder
1 teaspoon cummin powder
2 tomatoes, chopped
salt to taste
lemon juice to taste

Cut the meat into small cubes. Scrape the ginger, wash and cut into thin round slices. Slice 1 onion finely and cut the other into small pieces. Thread alternately cubes of meat, pieces of onion and slices of ginger on to a wooden cocktail stick until it is tightly packed. Continue in this way until all the meat is used up.

Grind the poppy seeds, garlic and coconut to a paste. Heat the ghee and fry the sliced onion till golden brown. Add the paste and other spices and fry for 3 minutes. Add the chopped tomatoes and cook for 5 minutes. Add 300 ml/½ pint water and salt and when boiling put in the meat sticks and simmer covered for 10 minutes. Add lemon juice to taste.

If you find the ginger too pungent, you can thread the sticks with onions and meat and just one or two slices of ginger.

HUSSAINY CURRY (2)

METRIC/IMPERIAL

1-kg/2-lb piece lean stewing mutton
3.5-cm/1½-inch piece green ginger
3 small onions
50 g/2 oz cooking fat
2 teaspoons cummin powder
2 teaspoons coriander powder
½ teaspoon chilli powder
½ teaspoon turmeric
1 tablespoon tomato purée
¼ teaspoon salt
4 tablespoons yogurt

Boil the mutton in one piece till fully cooked. Cut in small squares. Cut the green ginger and onions in rounds. Take a skewer and string on it one piece of onion, one of mutton and one of green ginger. Repeat until each skewer is filled. Place aside.

Now make the gravy of spices. Put the cooking fat into a pan and heat it. Mix the spices and tomato purée with 150 ml/¼ pint water. Put into the pan and fry, stirring all the time, until brown in colour. Season with salt.

Add the skewers of meat and the yogurt. Simmer gently for 10 to 15 minutes.

PORK CURRY

METRIC/IMPERIAL

450 g/1 lb lean pork
15 g/½ oz tamarind
2 medium onions
3 cloves garlic
50 g/2 oz cooking fat
3 tablespoons vinegar
2 teaspoons curry powder
½ teaspoon garam masala
2 teaspoons salt

Wash and cut pork into cubes. Soak the tamarind in 150 ml/¼ pint water for 10 minutes, then squeeze and strain the juice. Slice the onions finely. Slice the garlic.

Heat the fat and fry the onions until cream coloured. Add the tamarind water, the vinegar and garlic and fry. Add the meat and fry till well browned. Put in the curry powder and garam masala and fry for 3 minutes. Now add 300 ml/½ pint hot water and salt and simmer gently till the pork is tender.

If a sweet-sour curry is preferred, add ½ teaspoon sugar with the hot water. Serve with plain boiled rice.

KORMA CURRY
(Mutton, Beef or Lamb)

METRIC/IMPERIAL

450 g/1 lb lean meat
150 ml/¼ pint yogurt
2 large onions
2 tablespoons freshly grated or 1 tablespoon desiccated coconut
2 cloves garlic
1½ tablespoons poppy seeds
2.5-cm/1-inch piece ginger or ¼ teaspoon ginger powder
3 teaspoons coriander powder
¼ teaspoon ground cinnamon
¼ teaspoon ground cloves
1 teaspoon chilli powder
100 g/4 oz ghee
salt to taste
4 green chillies
a few sprigs of green coriander leaves (if available)
lemon juice to taste

Clean and cut the meat into 2.5-cm/1-inch pieces. Put the yogurt in a bowl and whisk till smooth. Slice the onions finely. Grind coconut, garlic, poppy seeds and ginger to a paste and mix in all the powdered spices.

Heat the ghee and fry the onions a crisp golden brown. Drain the onions and crush them. Put them in the yogurt. Add the paste to the ghee and fry over low heat for 5 minutes. Add meat, yogurt and salt; bring to the boil then simmer over low heat till the meat is tender and the curry is a rich brown.

Add the green chillies whole or sliced and the coriander leaves; put the lid on and remove from the heat.
Before serving add the lemon juice and more salt if required.

DRY MUTTON AND YOGURT CURRY

METRIC/IMPERIAL

2 cloves garlic (sliced)
450 g/1 lb lean mutton or other meat
1-cm/½-inch piece ginger
coriander seeds
cummin seeds
1 red chilli (broken in half)
40 g/1½ oz cooking fat
4 onions, sliced
1 teaspoon salt
½ teaspoon sugar
300 ml/½ pint yogurt

First soak the sliced garlic in 300 ml/½ pint water for 1 hour. Then cube the meat, put in a bowl and pour the soaked garlic water with the garlic over it; leave for 2 hours.

Next tie the sliced ginger, coriander seeds, cummin seeds and red chilli in a small muslin bag.

Heat the cooking fat and fry the onions to a light cream colour. Put in the meat and garlic water with garlic. Add the muslin bag and simmer till meat is tender, then add salt, sugar and yogurt.

Stir well and simmer without lid till nearly all liquid has evaporated.

DRY CURRY

METRIC/IMPERIAL

450 g/1 lb lean meat
100 g/4 oz freshly grated or 50 g/2 oz desiccated coconut
1 teaspoon poppy seeds
4 teaspoons coriander powder
1 teaspoon cummin powder
½ teaspoon chilli powder
½ teaspoon turmeric
3 cloves garlic
3 medium onions
4 tablespoons cooking fat
½ teaspoon ground cinnamon
1 teaspoon salt

Cut the meat into small cubes. Soak the coconut in 150 ml/¼ pint hot water for 10 minutes, then squeeze and strain the milk.

Warm the poppy seeds, coriander, cummin, chilli and turmeric in a dry frying pan and grind these spices with the garlic to a paste. Chop the onions.

Heat the fat and fry the onions a light brown. Now add the ground spices, cinnamon and salt and fry till rich brown, then add the coconut milk and another 150 ml/¼ pint water. Simmer gently till the meat is tender and the liquid has dried up.

Serve with plain boiled rice and lentil dal.

DRY MUTTON CURRY

METRIC/IMPERIAL

50 g/2 oz cooking fat
2 onions, sliced
½ teaspoon cummin seeds
1 teaspoon poppy seeds
¼ teaspoon chilli powder
3 cloves garlic
½ teaspoon turmeric
1 teaspoon mustard seeds
450 g/1 lb lean mutton or meat
1 tablespoon chopped coriander or watercress leaves
¼ green pepper, sliced
1 teaspoon salt

Heat cooking fat and fry onions till deep cream in colour. Add cummin seeds, poppy seeds, chilli, garlic, turmeric and mustard seeds, all ground together into the onions, and fry for 5 minutes.

Cut meat into cubes, add to the pan and brown well, continually stirring to keep it from burning. Add the coriander or watercress leaves and green pepper, stir and add salt and 450 ml/¾ pint hot water.

Simmer till meat is cooked and the gravy nearly gone.

STUFFED PEPPER CURRY

METRIC/IMPERIAL

4 medium green peppers

for stuffing:

1 medium onion
1 clove garlic
25 g/1 oz ghee or butter
225 g/8 oz lean minced meat
½ teaspoon ginger powder
½ teaspoon turmeric
1 teaspoon chilli powder
salt to taste
1 teaspoon garam masala

for curry:

1 medium onion
1 clove garlic
1 teaspoon chilli powder
1 teaspoon ginger powder
50 g/2 oz ghee or butter
¼ teaspoon cummin seeds
4 tablespoons yogurt
salt to taste

To make stuffing, chop the onion and garlic finely. Heat the 25 g/1 oz ghee and fry the onion and garlic till lightly browned. Add the mince, ginger, turmeric, chilli and salt and fry for 3–4 minutes till the mince is nicely browned. Add a little water and fry for 2–3 minutes more. Sprinkle with the garam masala and remove from the heat. Cool.

Slice the tops off the peppers and scoop out the seeds. Fill each cavity with the stuffing and put on the top. Secure with thin wooden cocktail sticks.

To make curry, grind onion and garlic to a paste and mix in chilli and ginger powders. Heat remaining ghee and fry the cummin seeds for 30 seconds, lower heat and add the paste. Fry for 3 minutes, then put in the peppers.

Beat the yogurt and add salt. Pour the yogurt over the peppers. Cover and simmer till the peppers are tender and the curry is a rich brown colour.

LIVER CURRY

METRIC/IMPERIAL

450 g/1 lb liver
4 small cloves garlic
2 green chillies
225 g/8 oz onions
225 g/8 oz tomatoes
50 g/2 oz ghee or butter
1 teaspoon turmeric
½ teaspoon ginger powder
salt to taste
2 tablespoons yogurt
1 teaspoon garam masala
1 teaspoon chilli powder

Wash and cut liver into 2.5-cm/1-inch pieces. Chop the garlic and green chillies. Slice onions into thickish rings. Slice the tomatoes.

Heat the ghee, add the onions, turmeric and tomatoes and fry till the mixture is a rich brown. Add the garlic, green chillies and ginger and fry for 2 minutes. Add the liver and salt and fry for 5 minutes. Add the yogurt, garam masala and chilli powder and fry for another 1–2 minutes.

Cover and simmer till the liver is cooked.

CURRIED BRAINS

METRIC/IMPERIAL

1 medium onion	¾ teaspoon turmeric
1 large tomato	½ teaspoon chilli powder
4 sheep's brains	3 teaspoons coriander powder
4 teaspoons vinegar	2 teaspoons salt
50 g/2 oz cooking fat	300 ml/½ pint yogurt
3 teaspoons cummin powder	

Slice onion finely. Slice tomato. Wash the brains and plunge them into boiling water. Drain, cool, remove membranes and veins and clean the brains. Cut them in half.

Place the brains in a saucepan with vinegar and enough cold water to cover and bring to the boil. Remove from heat, drain and reserve.

Heat the fat and fry the onion and tomato over a low heat till onions are cream coloured. Add the spices, salt and yogurt and simmer till the curry is thick. Add 300 ml/½ pint hot water and simmer for 10 minutes more. Add the brains and cook for 15 minutes.

MUTTON BUFFATH

METRIC/IMPERIAL

1 small leg mutton	2.5-cm/1-inch piece fresh ginger or ½ teaspoon ginger powder
4 onions	4 dried red chillies
4 medium potatoes	1 teaspoon turmeric
salt to taste	50 g/2 oz ghee or cooking fat
4 small carrots	1 medium onion, sliced finely
4 radishes or 2 parsnips	2–3 cloves
4 cloves garlic	5-cm/2-inch stick cinnamon
1 tablespoon cooked rice	1 tablespoon vinegar

Remove some of the fat from the leg of mutton. Boil the meat in a generous litre/2 pints water with the peeled whole onions and potatoes, salt, carrots and radishes. Simmer, after bringing to the boil. When the vegetables are tender, remove and reserve.

Grind the garlic, rice, ginger and chillies to a paste. Add the turmeric to the paste. Remove the meat when cooked and keep the stock aside.

Heat the ghee and fry the mutton till brown; remove the meat. Fry the finely sliced onion in the fat till light brown and fry the curry paste slightly. Pour in the stock with the cloves and cinnamon and bring to the boil. Add the vinegar and more salt if required.

Place the meat on a dish with the vegetables. Pour the gravy over and serve.

LIVER KABABS

METRIC/IMPERIAL

- 1 kg/2 lb lamb's liver
- juice of 2 lemons
- 2 teaspoons chilli powder
- salt to taste
- butter or oil for basting

Wash and dry liver and cut into 2.5-cm/1-inch pieces. Marinate the pieces in lemon juice, chilli powder and salt for 1 hour. Fix the liver on to skewers and grill gently on both sides. Baste with butter or oil. Serve with plain boiled rice.

DHANSAK
(Meat and Lentil Curry)

METRIC/IMPERIAL

- 1 kg/2 lb lean meat or 1 (1.5-kg/3½-lb) chicken
- 450 g/1 lb mixed dal consisting of 100 g/4 oz tuar dal and 75 g/3 oz each mung, chana and masoor dal
- 100 g/4 oz spinach
- 2 small aubergines
- 100 g/4 oz pumpkin or marrow (optional)
- 2 large potatoes
- 1 large onion
- 1 bunch spring onions (optional)
- 4 sprigs mint
- 4 tablespoons coriander or watercress leaves
- 1 large green pepper
- 2 teaspoons fenugreek seeds
- 2 teaspoons turmeric
- ½ tablespoon garam masala
- 4 teaspoons salt
- 225 g/8 oz butter or margarine
- 7 cloves garlic
- 2 teaspoons cummin powder
- 1 teaspoon chilli powder

Wash and cut meat into pieces (or joint chicken).

Wash and clean the dal and put in saucepan with meat.

Wash the spinach well, remove grit and chop coarsely. Peel and chop aubergine coarsely. If tinned, empty into saucepan with meat and dal. Peel and coarsely chop the marrow, potatoes, onion and spring onions. De-sprig the mint and coriander or watercress leaves and leave whole. Wash, deseed and chop the green pepper.

Add the cleaned and chopped ingredients to the dal and meat. Wash clean and add the fenugreek seeds (essential), the turmeric, garam masala, salt, 175 g/6 oz butter and 2 litres/3½ pints cold water.

Bring to the boil, cover, and simmer till meat and dal are soft and cooked. If more water is necessary, add *hot* water.

Remove pieces of meat and keep hot. Mash dal against side of saucepan with wooden spoon or in mouli sieve. Return dal and meat to saucepan.

Peel the cloves of garlic and mash well. Put the garlic into a small saucepan. Add the cummin and chilli. Add the remaining butter. Heat all together and fry. Add to the dal and meat and mix well. Bring to the boil just once, then remove from heat and serve hot.

Note: If the pepper or chilli and garlic are too much for European tastes, all these ingredients may be lessened in quantity. But a little must be used, otherwise the taste of the Dhansak will not be the same.

PARSEE MEAT BALLS

Oven temperature: Moderate
160°C, 325°F, Gas Mark 3

METRIC/IMPERIAL

4 onions
4 cloves garlic
1 teaspoon ginger powder
½ green pepper
4 eggs
1 kg/2 lb finely minced meat
1 teaspoon turmeric
4 teaspoons curry powder
½ teaspoon chilli powder
1 teaspoon ground cloves
1 tablespoon flour
salt to taste
4 tablespoons cooking fat

Chop the onions finely. Grind the garlic and mix with ginger.

Chop the green pepper. Beat the eggs. Mix with all the ingredients except the fat. Leave to stand for 3–4 hours.

Shape into balls the size of an egg and fry in the fat. Finish off cooking in the oven, until the meat balls are cooked right through.

MINCE CURRY

METRIC/IMPERIAL

5 large onions
¼ green pepper or 1 green chilli
2 tablespoons coriander leaves or 1 teaspoon coriander powder
3 cloves garlic
1 teaspoon ginger powder
450 g/1 lb finely minced meat
1 teaspoon turmeric
¼ teaspoon chilli powder
1 teaspoon cummin powder
100 g/4 oz cooking fat
salt to taste
½ teaspoon black pepper
1 tablespoon Worcestershire sauce
1 tablespoon tomato ketchup
1 teaspoon sugar

Chop the onions, green pepper or chilli and coriander leaves very finely. Grind or pound the garlic and mix with the ginger. Put the mince in a bowl.

With the pepper or chilli, coriander and half the onions, make into a paste with the garlic, turmeric, chilli powder and cummin.

Heat the fat and fry the remaining onions and the paste for 3–4 minutes. Add the mince, 450 ml/¾ pint warm water, salt and pepper. Cover and simmer till meat is cooked.

Add the Worcestershire sauce, tomato ketchup and sugar. Mix thoroughly. Remove from heat.

MINCED CUTLETS

METRIC/IMPERIAL

1 large potato
4 cloves garlic
1 large onion
1 green pepper
1 tablespoon chopped parsley
450 g/1 lb lean minced meat
¼ teaspoon turmeric
½ teaspoon ginger powder
1 teaspoon cummin powder
4 eggs
salt and pepper to taste
breadcrumbs
2 tablespoons oil

Boil and mash potato. Crush garlic cloves. Chop onion and green pepper. Add with the parsley to the mince in a bowl together with the spices and 1 egg. Mix thoroughly, preferably with the hand. Season to taste. Mix and leave for at least 1 hour.

When required beat together remaining 3 eggs. Take a quarter of mixture and shape into a cutlet. Dip in beaten egg and then in breadcrumbs.

Heat oil and fry the cutlets on medium heat till meat is cooked. Brown on both sides. Remove and keep hot till all the cutlets are cooked. Serve with tomato ketchup or sauce.

PARSEE MINCE

METRIC/IMPERIAL

6 large onions
1 green chilli
bunch coriander or watercress leaves (optional)
4 cloves garlic
1 teaspoon ginger powder
2 tablespoons cooking fat
450 g/1 lb lean minced meat
½ teaspoon turmeric
2 teaspoons cummin powder
salt to taste
4 tablespoons vinegar
2 teaspoons sugar

Slice 3 onions finely. Chop the remaining 3 onions. Chop the chilli and coriander leaves. Grind the garlic and mix in the ginger.

Heat the fat and fry the sliced onions golden brown. Lower heat, add the garlic paste and fry for 2 minutes. Add the mince, fry till nicely browned, then add the turmeric, cummin, chopped onions, chilli and coriander leaves.

Fry, then put in 450 ml/¾ pint water and salt. Bring to the boil, then simmer over low heat till the meat is cooked.

Mix the vinegar and sugar. When the liquid in the mince is dried add the vinegar mixture. Mix and serve.

KEEMA MATAR
(Mince with Peas)

METRIC/IMPERIAL

2 medium onions
1 clove garlic
75 g/3 oz ghee
450 g/1 lb minced meat
1 teaspoon turmeric
1 teaspoon chilli powder
½ teaspoon ginger powder
salt to taste
4 tablespoons yogurt
225 g/8 oz shelled peas
1 teaspoon garam masala
a few sprigs of coriander leaves (optional)
2 green chillies, chopped
lemon juice (optional)

Slice the onions finely and chop the garlic.

Heat the fat and fry the onions a golden brown. Lower the heat slightly and add the garlic, mince, turmeric, chilli, ginger and salt. Fry for 5 minutes, then add the yogurt. Mix thoroughly, cover and simmer till mince is nearly cooked. Add the peas, cover and simmer till both mince and peas are tender. If too dry when cooking, add a tablespoon of water as often as necessary.

Sprinkle with garam masala, chopped coriander leaves and green chillies. Lemon juice may be added if preferred.

SPICY AND SOUR MEAT

METRIC/IMPERIAL

450 g/1 lb meat
3 cloves garlic
2 medium onions, sliced
½ teaspoon garam masala
¼ teaspoon ginger powder
½ teaspoon turmeric
2 teaspoons cummin powder
3 tablespoons vinegar
25 g/1 oz cooking fat
4 tablespoons water

Cut meat in cubes. Mash garlic cloves and mix with sliced onion, spices and 2 tablespoons vinegar. Heat the cooking fat and fry the mixture for 5 minutes, stirring constantly.

Put in the meat cubes and fry until brown, stirring constantly to prevent burning. Add the rest of the vinegar to the water and pour into the fried meat and spices. Cover and simmer on a very low heat till meat is tender.

Stir occasionally so that meat does not burn.

POTATO CHOPS WITH MINCE

METRIC/IMPERIAL

1 kg/2 lb potatoes
1 medium onion
1-cm/½-inch
piece fresh ginger or
¼ teaspoon ginger powder
2 green chillies
a few mint leaves
450 g/1 lb cold roast meat
1 tablespoon ghee or
butter
salt and pepper to taste
2 eggs, beaten
breadcrumbs
fat for frying

Peel and boil potatoes. Mash till quite smooth and free from lumps and season with salt. Chop the onion, ginger, chillies and mint. Mince the meat.

Heat the ghee and fry the onion till golden brown; add the chillies, mint, mince and ginger. Season with salt and pepper. Fry for 2 minutes till well mixed, then cool.

Take a tablespoon of potato and make into an oval shape. Make a hollow in the centre and fill with mince mixture; cover with potato. Dip in beaten egg, coat with breadcrumbs and fry till pale gold.

Serve with tomato sauce and boiled vegetables.

KOFTAS
(Meat Balls)

METRIC/IMPERIAL

¼ green pepper
1 medium onion
450 g/1 lb finely minced
meat
2½ tablespoons yogurt
1½ teaspoons salt
2 tablespoons coriander
or watercress leaves
1 teaspoon garam masala
fat for frying

Chop the green pepper and onion very finely. Mix with the other ingredients (except the fat) in a bowl. Shape the mixture into tiny balls the size of marbles.

Heat the fat in a frying pan and deep fry the meat balls. These koftas can be served on cocktail sticks with drinks or added to fried rice.

AUBERGINES STUFFED WITH MINCE

Oven temperature: Moderate
160°C, 325°F, Gas Mark 3

METRIC/IMPERIAL

4 medium or 2 large aubergines
salt
2 medium tomatoes
1 large onion
1 green pepper
1 green chilli
1-cm/½-inch piece fresh ginger
50–75 g/2–3 oz butter
2 tablespoons soft breadcrumbs
100 g/4 oz minced meat
salt and pepper to taste

Put the whole aubergines in boiling salted water and boil till barely tender. Cool and cut in half. Scoop out the pulp very carefully so as not to break the skin. Keep the skins for filling.

Skin and chop the tomatoes. Chop the onion, pepper, chilli and ginger.

Heat the butter and fry the breadcrumbs. Remove and set aside. In the same butter fry the onion and add the mince, ginger, chilli and green pepper and fry for 2–3 minutes. Add the aubergine pulp, tomatoes, salt, pepper and 1 tablespoon water and simmer gently till the mince is tender.

Fill the aubergine skins with the mince mixture. Smooth the tops and spread with fried crumbs. Put in the oven for 10 minutes to heat through, and serve.

STEWED MEAT BALLS

METRIC/IMPERIAL

450 g/1 lb minced meat
1 egg
2 large onions
1 green chilli
50 g/2 oz cooking fat
1 teaspoon ginger powder
1 teaspoon turmeric
1 teaspoon cummin powder
2 teaspoons coriander powder
¼ teaspoon chilli powder
pinch of mace
1 teaspoon garam masala
2 teaspoons salt

Mix the mince and egg together and form into small walnut size balls. Slice 1 onion finely. Mince the other onion and the green chilli.

Heat the fat and fry all the onions a light brown. Add all the spices and salt and fry gently for 5–6 minutes. Add the meat balls and fry till they are brown. Pour in 150 ml/¼ pint hot water and shake the saucepan gently. Simmer over low heat till the gravy is thick.

FRIED MINCE BALLS

METRIC/IMPERIAL

450 g/1 lb minced meat
1 medium onion
2 medium potatoes
¼ green pepper
1 tablespoon coriander leaves or 1 teaspoon coriander powder
1 teaspoon cummin powder
1 teaspoon garam masala
1 teaspoon salt
100 g/4 oz rice flour
fat for frying

Boil the mince in a little water. Chop the onion finely. Boil the potatoes, peel and mash them. Chop the green pepper and coriander leaves.

Put the mince in a bowl, add all the ingredients except the flour and fat and mix thoroughly. Roll into balls the size of small eggs. Coat with rice flour and fry over gentle heat until brown.

SPICED CRUMB CHOPS

Oven temperature: Hot
220°C, 425°F, Gas Mark 7

METRIC/IMPERIAL

8 lamb chops
4 cloves garlic
½ teaspoon ginger powder
¼ teaspoon chilli powder
¼ teaspoon cummin powder
1 teaspoon coriander powder
25 g/1 oz vinegar
2 teaspoons salt
2 eggs, beaten
breadcrumbs
50 g/2 oz cooking fat

Place chops between clean tea towels and pound with meat bat. Grind or mince the garlic very finely. Mix the garlic and spices with the vinegar. Add salt and the chops and leave to marinate for 4 hours.

Dip the chops in beaten egg and then in the breadcrumbs. Fry in the fat till brown then put into a casserole. Cover and place in the oven for 10 minutes.

GRILLED KABABS

METRIC/IMPERIAL

450 g/1 lb lamb shoulder
225 g/8 oz lamb fat
salt and pepper to taste
75 g/3 oz butter
juice of 1 lemon

Cut meat in 2.5-cm/1-inch cubes. Cut the fat in small thin slices to equal the amount of meat cubes. Sprinkle meat and fat with salt and pepper.

Melt butter, but do not let it boil. Dip the cubes of meat in butter. Arrange cubes on skewers; first a bit of meat then a slice of fat. Repeat until skewer is full, ending with a cube of meat. Grill under a hot grill, turning as necessary to brown all sides.

When ready sprinkle with lemon juice, and serve hot.

Note: Slices of bacon can be substituted for lamb fat, in which case do not salt the bacon.

KOFTA CURRY (1)
(Meat Balls)

METRIC/IMPERIAL

for koftas:

450 g/1 lb minced meat
1 teaspoon garam masala
1 egg
salt to taste
½ teaspoon ginger powder
1 teaspoon chilli powder or 1 green chilli, ground finely

for curry:

2 onions
2 cloves garlic
100 g/4 oz ghee
1 teaspoon turmeric
1 teaspoon ginger powder
2 teaspoons chilli powder
salt to taste
4 tablespoons yogurt

To make the koftas, mix all the ingredients thoroughly together. Shape into balls the size of a plum.

For the curry, chop the onions and grind the garlic to a paste.

Heat the ghee and put in the onions. Fry till the onions are half cooked. Add the garlic and fry for 2 minutes. Add the rest of the spices and salt and fry for 3 minutes. Beat the yogurt and add to the curry. Cover and simmer for 10 minutes till the sauce is smooth. Add 150 ml/¼ pint warm water and bring to the boil.

Put in the meat balls and simmer for 30 minutes. Serve with rice or bread.

KOFTA CURRY (2)
(Meat Balls)

METRIC/IMPERIAL

for koftas:

2 teaspoons mint leaves
1 medium onion
2 cloves garlic
450 g/1 lb finely minced meat
2 teaspoons salt
¼ teaspoon chilli powder
¼ teaspoon ground cloves
¼ teaspoon ginger powder

for curry:

2.5-cm/1-inch piece fresh ginger
1 tomato
2 cloves garlic
½ teaspoon ginger powder
1 medium onion
50 g/2 oz cooking fat
600 ml/1 pint yogurt
2 teaspoons coriander powder

To make the koftas, chop the mint finely. Chop the onion and 2 cloves garlic. Put the mince in a bowl with the mint, chopped garlic and onion. Mix and add the salt, chilli, clove and ginger powders. Make into balls the size of a large walnut.

For the curry, scrape the ginger and chop very finely. Chop the tomato coarsely, crush the garlic and add to 150 ml/¼ pint water and the ginger powder. Slice the onion finely.

Heat the fat and fry onion till cream coloured. Add the tomato, yogurt and coriander powder and simmer for 15 minutes. Add the garlic water, simmer for 5 minutes and add the meat balls. Cover and cook gently till the meat is cooked.

If more gravy is required, add 150 ml/¼ pint hot water and simmer for 5 minutes more. Serve with rice or bread.

KOFTA CURRY KASHMIRI

METRIC/IMPERIAL

- 3 green chillies
- 675 g/1½ lb lean minced meat
- 3 tablespoons yogurt
- 1 teaspoon ginger powder
- ½ teaspoon coriander powder
- 1 teaspoon chilli powder
- 2 teaspoons garam masala
- 100 g/4 oz ghee
- salt to taste
- 1 teaspoon sugar
- 1 tablespoon dried milk
- 1 teaspoon black pepper
- 2 green cardamoms, ground coarsely

Chop the green chillies very finely. Put the mince in a bowl and add the chopped chillies, 1 tablespoon yogurt, ginger, coriander, chilli, 1 teaspoon garam masala, 25 g/1 oz ghee and salt to taste. Mix thoroughly and shape into small sausages.

Heat the rest of the ghee in a saucepan; add the sugar, dried milk, 2 tablespoons yogurt, 1 teaspoon garam masala and salt to taste. Fry for 1 minute and add 150 ml/¼ pint warm water and the meat koftas. Simmer till the water is dry then turn the koftas and add another 150 ml/¼ pint warm water. Simmer till water is absorbed.

Sprinkle with black pepper and the cardamoms.

PORK VINDALOO

METRIC/IMPERIAL

- 3 large onions
- 5 cloves garlic
- 2 large cardamoms
- 8 cloves
- 20 peppercorns
- 3 tablespoons vinegar
- 3 teaspoons chilli powder
- 1 teaspoon ground cinnamon
- 2 teaspoons cummin powder
- 2 teaspoons turmeric
- 2 teaspoons dry mustard
- 1 teaspoon ginger powder or 5-cm/2-inch piece fresh ginger
- 1 kg/2 lb pork
- salt to taste
- 4 tablespoons mustard oil

Grind 2 onions, garlic, cardamom seeds, cloves and peppercorns to a paste with a little vinegar. Mix into this paste all the powdered spices; add a little more vinegar to keep moist.

Wash, dry and cut the pork into 3.5-cm/1½-inch pieces. Put the meat into a bowl and marinate with a quarter of the paste and salt to taste. Pour the rest of the vinegar over the meat and leave for 5–6 hours.

Slice the remaining onion finely. If fresh ginger is used, scrape, wash and cut into slices. Heat the oil till it smokes, then cool.

Put on a medium heat and fry the onions and ginger slices till light brown, add the remaining paste and fry till the raw smell disappears. Add the pork mixture and simmer over a low heat till the meat is tender.

This is a very hot curry and can be kept for a few days. No water must be used when cooking the vindaloo.

DAL GOSHT
(Lentil and Meat)

METRIC/IMPERIAL

100 g/4 oz chana dal
450 g/1 lb lean meat
2 medium onions
2 cloves garlic
1 teaspoon turmeric
1 teaspoon cummin powder
1 teaspoon coriander powder
½ teaspoon ginger powder
1 teaspoon chilli powder
100 g/4 oz ghee
1 teaspoon garam masala
1 bay leaf
2.5-cm/1-inch stick cinnamon
3 tablespoons yogurt
salt to taste

Wash and soak dal in water for 3 hours before cooking. Cut the meat into 2.5-cm/1-inch pieces. Slice 1 onion finely. Grind the other onion and the garlic to a paste. Mix into the paste all the powdered spices and if too dry add a little water.

Heat ghee and fry the sliced onion a golden brown. Lower heat and add the garam masala, bay leaf and cinnamon and fry for 2 minutes. Add the meat and yogurt and mix thoroughly. Add salt and simmer till the liquid is nearly gone. Add the drained dal and fry for 2–3 minutes then put in 300 ml/½ pint water.

Bring to the boil and simmer over low heat, covered, till the dal and meat are tender.

ALU GOSHT
(Potatoes and Meat)

METRIC/IMPERIAL

450 g/1 lb potatoes
100 g/4 oz ghee
2 large onions
2–3 cloves garlic
½ teaspoon ginger or 2.5-cm/1-inch piece fresh ginger
1 kg/2 lb lean meat
4 tablespoons yogurt
2 teaspoons coriander powder
2 teaspoons chilli powder
1 teaspoon turmeric
1 teaspoon cummin powder
2 teaspoons paprika
1 teaspoon garam masala
1 bay leaf
salt to taste

Use equal size potatoes. Peel and wash them; if large cut them in half or quarters. Dry the potatoes and fry in ghee till lightly browned. Drain and keep aside.

Slice 1 onion finely. Grind the other onion, garlic, and ginger to a paste. Wash the meat, then cut into 2.5-cm/1-inch pieces. Beat the yogurt till smooth. Add all the powdered spices to the paste and if too dry add a little water.

Heat the ghee remaining in the pan and fry the sliced onion a golden brown. Lower heat and fry the bay leaf and the paste for 2 minutes. Add the meat and fry for 3–4 minutes till the meat is slightly browned. Add the yogurt and salt, mix thoroughly and simmer covered till the meat is nearly cooked. Add the potatoes and 4 tablespoons warm water and simmer till the potatoes are tender. Remove bay leaf.

BEEF DO-PIAZA WITH EGGS

METRIC/IMPERIAL

1 kg/2 lb beef
675 g/1½ lb onions
2 cloves garlic
100 g/4 oz ghee
1 teaspoon turmeric
2 teaspoons chilli powder
2 teaspoons coriander powder
salt to taste
1½ teaspoon garam masala
2 green cardamoms
2 bay leaves
1 small stick cinnamon
4 eggs
1 tablespoon vinegar

Cut the meat into 3.5-cm/1½-inch pieces. Slice 225 g/8 oz of the onions finely. Chop the rest of the onions and the garlic.

Heat the ghee and fry the sliced onions until golden brown. Remove the pan from the heat and add to the fried onions and ghee the meat, chopped onions, turmeric, chilli, coriander, salt and 3 tablespoons hot water. Simmer till dry.

Add the chopped garlic and fry, stirring all the time, till the onions are pulpy and mixed with the gravy. Add another 3 tablespoons hot water, garam masala, cardamoms, bay leaves and cinnamon and simmer again till nearly dry.

Slip each egg very carefully into the curry; cook over a very low heat. Add vinegar and cook until the eggs are done.

DO-PIAZA

METRIC/IMPERIAL

675 g/1½ lb meat
675 g/1½ lb onions
3 cloves garlic
2.5-cm/1-inch piece fresh ginger or ½ teaspoon ginger powder
450 ml/¾ pint yogurt
2 teaspoons coriander seeds
1 teaspoon turmeric
1 teaspoon cummin seeds
½ teaspoon cloves
10-cm/4-inch stick cinnamon
10 dried red chillies
2 bay leaves
½ teaspoon peppercorns
4 large cardamoms
salt to taste
50 g/2 oz ghee or butter

Clean and cut meat into small pieces. Cut onions into quarters. Chop the garlic finely and scrape, wash and slice the fresh ginger. Beat the yogurt till smooth.

Put all the ingredients except the ghee in a saucepan with a tight-fitting lid. Mix well and cover. Bring gently to the boil and simmer till all the liquid is absorbed. If the meat is not cooked add a little water and cook again till dry.

Add the ghee and fry the curry. Stir very carefully so as not to break up the meat. Serve with chapatis.

MEAT CUBE SKEWERED KABABS

METRIC/IMPERIAL

1 teaspoon powdered poppy seeds
1 teaspoon ginger powder
2 teaspoons coriander powder
1 teaspoon turmeric
¼ teaspoon chilli powder
1 teaspoon salt
1 teaspoon onion juice (see page 18)
2 teaspoons yogurt
450 g/1 lb meat, cut in cubes
25 g/1 oz melted cooking fat

Mix all the spices and salt, including the onion juice. Add the yogurt. Soak the meat in boiling water for 5 minutes, then remove and drain it. Mix the meat well with the yogurt and spices. See that all the cubes are well coated. Leave for 30 minutes.

Thread the cubes on metal skewers. Grill under a preheated grill and baste continuously with the melted fat till done. Grill gently so that meat is tender and cooked through.

Collect the gravy which forms at the bottom of the pan and serve with the grilled meat.

BAKED KABAB

Oven temperature: Moderately hot
190°C, 375°F, Gas Mark 5

METRIC/IMPERIAL

50 g/2 oz gram or wholewheat flour
2 onions
2 cloves garlic
2 green chillies
1 teaspoon chilli powder
½ teaspoon ground cloves
½ teaspoon ginger powder
½ teaspoon ground cinnamon
1 teaspoon garam masala
450 g/1 lb minced beef or lamb
1 tablespoon yogurt or lemon juice
salt and pepper to taste
15 g/½ oz butter
few mint leaves

Roast the gram flour in a dry frying pan till it is lightly browned. Chop finely the onions, garlic and green chillies. Mix all the spices, chopped ingredients, gram flour, mince, yogurt or lemon juice, salt and pepper together thoroughly.

Grease a casserole with the butter and put in the mince. Sprinkle with mint leaves, cover and cook in the oven for 45 minutes, then take off the lid and cook uncovered for another 15 minutes when the kabab should be ready.

SHIKAMPOORIE KABABS

METRIC/IMPERIAL

- 1 medium onion
- 2 cloves garlic
- 2–3 green chillies
- 1-cm/½-inch piece fresh ginger or ¼ teaspoon ginger powder
- 2 tablespoons yogurt
- 2 teaspoons freshly grated coconut
- ghee or cooking fat for frying
- ½ teaspoon cummin powder
- ¼ teaspoon cardamom powder
- ½ teaspoon garam masala
- 1 teaspoon turmeric
- 1 teaspoon coriander powder
- ¼ teaspoon ground cinnamon
- pinch of ground cloves
- ½ teaspoon ground almonds
- 1 tablespoon gram flour
- 450 g/1 lb lean minced meat
- salt to taste
- a few sprigs of mint

Chop the onion, garlic, chillies and fresh ginger very finely. The meat must be very finely minced and very lean. Tie the yogurt in a clean piece of muslin and hang up to drip. Soak the coconut in 1 tablespoon hot water for 10 minutes, then squeeze and strain.

Melt 1 tablespoon ghee and fry the onion, garlic, chillies and ginger for 4 minutes. Add the other spices and almonds and cook for another 4 minutes, stirring all the time. Add the gram flour, mince (which should be very finely minced and very lean), coconut milk and salt to taste. Stir and cook for 10 minutes.

Cool, then put into an electric blender or grinder and grind till the mixture is a very fine paste. Chop the mint leaves very finely and mix with the yogurt curds, which should be like cream cheese. Add salt to this mixture.

Take small balls of mince, depress in the centre and put ¼ teaspoon yogurt mixture in the middle. Work the mince over the filling and flatten the kabab. Make as many as possible then fry in shallow fat on both sides till brown.

SEEKH KABABS (1)

METRIC/IMPERIAL

1 kg/2 lb lean meat
25 g/1 oz poppy seeds
2 cloves garlic
1 large onion, chopped
2 teaspoons garam masala
¼ teaspoon grated nutmeg
salt to taste
1 tablespoon sweet oil
melted butter (if required)

Cut the meat into long narrow strips 1.5 cm/¾ inch wide and 15 cm/6 inches long. Grind the poppy seeds, garlic and onion to a paste. Add the garam masala, nutmeg and salt to the paste.

Marinate the meat in the oil and paste for 1 hour or more. Thread the strips on to skewers. Grill. Baste with butter if necessary.

Serve with chapatis or parathas.

SEEKH KABABS (2)

METRIC/IMPERIAL

1 lemon
1 onion
1 tomato
1 egg
450 g/1 lb very finely minced meat
1 teaspoon coriander powder
½ teaspoon cummin powder
¼ teaspoon chilli powder
½ teaspoon garam masala
1 teaspoon salt
40 g/1½ oz cooking fat

Slice the lemon in rounds, removing pips. Slice onion in rings and separate them. Scald, skin and slice tomato. Set these aside.

Mix the egg and mince well in a bowl. Add the spices and salt. Apply some grease to fingers and skewers, and fold meat in a long cigar shape evenly on to skewers. Brush well with cooking fat and grill gently under low grill in greased grilling pan. Turn skewers often so that meat is browned evenly all over.

When kababs are ready slide them gently off skewers so that they do not break. Serve at once in a hot dish with the lemon slices, onion rings and tomato slices arranged around them.

MINCE KABABS

METRIC/IMPERIAL

1 onion	450 g/1 lb lean minced meat
3 cloves garlic	¼ teaspoon chilli powder
¼ green pepper or 2 green chillies	½ teaspoon salt
bunch coriander or watercress	¼ teaspoon pepper
2 large slices crustless bread	1½ teaspoons Worcestershire sauce
	½ teaspoon dry mustard
	50 g/2 oz cooking fat

Chop the onion, garlic, green pepper and coriander very finely. Soak the bread in cold water for 5 minutes then squeeze out the water. Mix all the ingredients, except the fat, in a bowl. Mix thoroughly with the hand, kneading well, then shape into small balls and flatten slightly.

Heat the fat and fry over a low heat so that the meat is cooked while frying until brown.

KABABS MINCED A LA KABUL

METRIC/IMPERIAL

1 large onion	½ teaspoon ginger powder
½ green pepper	½ teaspoon garam masala
1 tablespoon coriander or watercress leaves	1 teaspoon salt
10 almonds	450 g/1 lb finely minced lean meat
50 g/2 oz cooking fat	25 g/1 oz gram flour
15 g/½ oz desiccated coconut	

Grind or chop very finely the onion, green pepper, coriander leaves and almonds.

Heat 15 g/½ oz cooking fat and fry the ground ingredients, coconut, ginger, garam masala and salt. Add the mince and 3 tablespoons hot water and simmer gently till the liquid is quite gone. Stir often so that the contents do not burn. Cool.

Make walnut size balls of the mixture, coat with gram flour and flatten into round cakes. Heat the remaining fat and fry the kababs till crisp and brown.

SHAMI KABABS (1)

METRIC/IMPERIAL

1 kg/2 lb lean mince	4 dried red chillies
2 cloves garlic	2 bay leaves
2 onions	salt to taste
8 peppercorns	100 g/4 oz chana dal
6 cloves	3 eggs
5-cm/2-inch stick cinnamon	2 green chillies
½ teaspoon ginger powder	few sprigs of mint
3 large cardamoms	ghee for frying
¼ teaspoon shah zeera (black cummin seeds)	

Boil together in 600 ml/1 pint water the mince, chopped garlic, 1 onion quartered, peppercorns, cloves, cinnamon, ginger, cardamoms, shah zeera, red chillies, bay leaves, salt and chana dal (washed). Simmer till the mixture is dry and the dal and meat are tender. Cool.

Remove the cinnamon stick, bay leaves and the cardamoms. Grind the meat mixture to a paste and mix with the 3 eggs. Chop very finely the remaining onion, green chillies and some mint leaves. Mix the chopped ingredients together.

Take tablespoonfuls of paste and make flat round cakes with ½ teaspoonfuls of the onion mixture in the centre. Cover the onion and pat the cakes into rounds about 1 cm/½ inch thick.

Fry in a little fat until cooked and brown.

SHAMI KABABS (2)

METRIC/IMPERIAL

450 g/1 lb minced meat	2 onions
100 g/4 oz dal	5-mm/¼-inch piece ginger
½ teaspoon ginger powder	3 cloves garlic
1 teaspoon coriander powder	1 tablespoon coriander or watercress leaves
½ teaspoon turmeric	
1 teaspoon cummin powder	3 mint leaves
½ teaspoon chilli powder	¼ green pepper
½ teaspoon garam masala	1 lemon
1 teaspoon salt	50 g/2 oz cooking fat

Boil meat and dal separately and grind or mince finely together. Mince or mix to a paste with 2 teaspoons water the ginger, coriander, turmeric, cummin, chilli, garam masala and salt. Mix in well with meat and dal.

Chop very finely and keep separate 1 onion, ginger, garlic, coriander or watercress leaves, mint leaves and green pepper.

Cut the other onion in rings and separate them. Slice lemon in rounds and remove seeds.

Make balls the size of large walnuts from the meat mixture. Form a depression and fill with the chopped ingredients, close over filling and flatten gently so that the chopped filling does not come out.

Heat cooking fat in frying pan and gently fry the flat kababs till done and brown. Serve at once with slices of lemon arranged around them and the onion rings over them.

PASAND KEEMA KABAB

METRIC/IMPERIAL

450 ml/¾ pint yogurt
25 g/1 oz green ginger or
  1 teaspoon ginger powder
1 kg/2 lb lean meat
4 green chillies
2 onions
100 g/4 oz ghee
1 teaspoon turmeric
1 teaspoon ground cloves
2 teaspoons pepper
salt to taste

Put the yogurt in a clean cloth, gather ends and tie up. Hang the cloth so that all the liquid is drained from the yogurt. Grind the green ginger and squeeze out the juice. Grind the meat in an electric blender or mince it very finely. Chop the chillies. Slice the onions finely and fry to a golden brown in the ghee. Remove the onions from the pan and drain.

Add to the mince the browned onions, ginger juice or powder, turmeric, chillies, cloves, pepper, salt and the drained yogurt. Mix all together and leave to marinate for 2 hours.

Heat the grill. Make sausages or balls of the mince mixture and pass skewers through them. Brush with melted butter or ghee and cook under grill, turning often.

FRIED LIVER

METRIC/IMPERIAL

450 g/1 lb liver
1 medium onion
2 cloves garlic
1 green chilli
15 g/½ oz vinegar
½ teaspoon turmeric
4 peppercorns, ground
½ teaspoon ginger powder
¼ teaspoon chilli powder
½ teaspoon cummin powder
2 teaspoons salt
juice of ½ lemon
25 g/1 oz fat

Wash, dry and slice the liver. Mince the onion, garlic and green chilli and mix in the vinegar. Add also the turmeric, pepper, ginger, chilli, cummin, salt and lemon juice. Marinate the liver pieces in the spices and leave for at least 1 hour.

Heat the fat and fry the liver very gently till cooked. Serve with mashed potatoes.

SPICED FRIED CHOPS (1)

METRIC/IMPERIAL

1 teaspoon ginger powder
¼ teaspoon chilli powder
1 teaspoon salt
1 teaspoon garlic salt
½ teaspoon sugar
1 tablespoon vinegar
8 lamb or mutton chops
4 medium potatoes
2 medium onions
50 g/2 oz cooking fat

Mix the ginger, chilli, salt, garlic salt and sugar with vinegar. Marinate the chops in this mixture, put a weight over the meat and leave for 4 hours.

Boil the potatoes, cool, peel and cut in round slices. Slice the onions finely and fry in the fat till crisp and golden. Remove and reserve.

Fry the chops till brown. Remove.

In the same fat fry the potatoes. Arrange the fried chops in a dish with potatoes in the centre and onions sprinkled over the meat. Serve with tomato sauce.

SPICED FRIED CHOPS (2)

METRIC/IMPERIAL

4 large potatoes
1 onion
2 cloves garlic
½ green pepper
6 mint leaves
1 tablespoon coriander or watercress leaves
8 lamb chops
2 teaspoons poppy seeds
¼ teaspoon turmeric
1 teaspoon ginger powder
1 teaspoon cummin powder
½ teaspoon garam masala
2 teaspoons salt
50 g/2 oz cooking fat
4 tomatoes

Peel the potatoes and cut in half. Slice the onion finely. Mince the garlic, green pepper, mint and coriander leaves.

Put the chops and potatoes in a saucepan and just cover with water. Boil, then simmer till liquid is dry. Add the minced garlic, leaves, green pepper, poppy seeds, powdered spices and salt and cook for 5 minutes. Keep shaking the pan so as to distribute the spices over the meat and potatoes. Remove the potatoes.

Heat the fat and fry the onions. Remove the onions. Halve the tomatoes and fry in the hot fat. Remove. Fry the potatoes and drain. Now fry the chops till they are brown.

Serve hot with tomatoes and onion in the middle and the potatoes round the chops. A tossed salad goes well with this dish.

HOT MUTTON STEW

METRIC/IMPERIAL

675 g/1½ lb mutton
4 large potatoes
3 large onions
2 teaspoons garam masala
½ teaspoon dry mustard
2 teaspoons salt
75 g/3 oz cooking fat
225 g/8 oz stock

Wash, dry and cut meat into large cubes. Peel and halve the potatoes. Peel and quarter the onions. Mix the garam masala, mustard and salt and rub into the mutton pieces. Leave for 1 hour.

Heat the cooking fat in a saucepan and fry the meat, onions and potatoes lightly. Add the stock and simmer till the meat is tender. Serve hot with chapatis.

CASSEROLE MEAT AND RICE

Oven temperature: Hot
220°C, 425°F, Gas Mark 7

METRIC/IMPERIAL

675 g/1½ lb meat
6 cloves garlic
675 g/1½ lb onions
350 g/12 oz rice
1 teaspoon turmeric
1 tablespoon garam masala
2 teaspoons ginger powder
1 teaspoon chilli powder
2 teaspoons sugar
2 teaspoons salt
300 ml/½ pint yogurt
175 g/6 oz ghee or butter
juice of 3 lemons
generous pinch saffron strands

Wash and cut meat into large pieces. Pound the garlic and chop the onions finely. Wash and parboil the rice. Drain and reserve.

Put the meat, garlic, turmeric, garam masala, ginger, chilli, sugar, salt and yogurt in a saucepan. Mix thoroughly and cook over medium heat till the meat is almost tender.

Heat the ghee and fry the onions until crisp and brown. Put a layer of rice in a casserole, then a layer of meat and gravy and onions, then the rice, and so on. Add the lemon juice and saffron strands. Cover with tight-fitting lid and put into the oven for 20 minutes.

Mix carefully and serve.

POTATO, ONION AND MEAT STEW

METRIC/IMPERIAL

450 g/1 lb meat
450 g/1 lb small onions
1 large onion
4 large potatoes
75 g/3 oz cooking fat
½ teaspoon garlic powder
½ teaspoon chilli powder
½ teaspoon ginger powder
½ teaspoon sugar
juice of ½ lemon

Cut meat into 3.5-cm/1½-inch pieces. Peel the small onions and slice the large one. Peel and quarter the potatoes and fry them in the fat. Keep them warm. Fry the small whole onions till they are a deep cream colour. Drain and keep warm. Fry the sliced onion.

Make the garlic, chilli and ginger powders into a paste with a little water. Add this paste to the onions and fry till brown. Now add the meat. Fry, turning constantly so that it does not stick or burn. Add 450 ml/¾ pint hot water when the meat is a rich brown.

Simmer till the meat is almost tender, then add the small onions and simmer till meat is tender. Pour the sugar, dissolved in the lemon juice, on the stew and cook for 5 minutes, then add potatoes to serve.

MULLIGATAWNY SOUP

METRIC/IMPERIAL

2 large onions
1 kg/2 lb stewing lamb
300 ml/½ pint milk
50 g/2 oz desiccated coconut
2 tablespoons ghee
1 teaspoon turmeric
¼ teaspoon cloves
1 teaspoon black pepper
3 teaspoons coriander powder
1 teaspoon cummin powder
¼ teaspoon ground cinnamon
2 tablespoons tomato purée
salt to taste
1 lemon, sliced

Slice onions. Cut the lamb into pieces. Cover with water and bring to the boil. Simmer till cooked. Strain, keep the stock and separate the meat from the bones. Discard the bones and keep the meat.

In a small pan put the milk, the coconut and 300 ml/½ pint water. Bring to the boil and simmer till the liquid is reduced to half. Strain.

Melt ghee and fry the onions in a large pan till they are golden brown. Add all the spices and the tomato purée and cook gently till well blended for 10 minutes. Add stock and the pieces of meat and bring to the boil once. Take off the heat. Season with salt.

Just before serving add the coconut milk. Reheat but do not boil. Serve with boiled rice and lemon slices.

KIDNEY CURRY

METRIC/IMPERIAL

6–8 kidneys
2 onions
2 tomatoes
3 cloves garlic
50 g/2 oz cooking fat
¼ teaspoon chilli powder
2 teaspoons curry powder
½ teaspoon garam masala
300 ml/½ pint yogurt
1 teaspoon salt

Wash kidneys well, remove skin and cut in half. Slice onions and tomatoes and chop the garlic.

Heat the fat and fry the onions until brown. Add the tomatoes, the spices and yogurt. Add salt and simmer over a gentle heat. Stir well, then add 600 ml/1 pint hot water and the kidneys.

Simmer gently, covered, until the kidneys are cooked.

SPICED BRAINS WITH SPINACH

METRIC/IMPERIAL

6 sheep's brains
3 tablespoons vinegar
3 teaspoons salt
15 g/½ oz tamarind
4 large onions
3 cloves garlic
1 green chilli or ½ green pepper
450 g/1 lb spinach
225 g/8 oz spring onions
bunch of coriander leaves
50 g/2 oz cooking fat
1 teaspoon cummin powder

Soak the brains in cold water with 2 tablespoons vinegar and 2½ teaspoons salt for 20 minutes. Wash the brains in clean water and boil in water to cover with 1 tablespoon vinegar and ½ teaspoon salt. Cool, remove skin and veins and cut into halves.

Soak the tamarind in 150 ml/¼ pint water and strain the juice. Slice the onions finely. Chop the garlic and green chilli. Wash the spinach and spring onions. Chop the spring onions, spinach and coriander leaves. Simmer in the fat over low heat, add sliced onions, green chilli, cummin, salt and tamarind water. Simmer till the spinach is cooked, then add the brains. Stir gently and serve.

Poultry

Although mostly chicken and duck recipes have been given in this book, the same recipes can be used for cooking game birds. Pheasants, partridges and quails are very popular.

One of the most favoured dishes at feasts and banquets is Murgh Mussallam – whole roasted, elaborately spiced chicken.

MURGH MUSSALLAM

METRIC/IMPERIAL

1 (1.5-kg/3-lb) chicken
3 large onions
4 cloves garlic
1 tablespoon poppy seeds
2 black cardamoms
½ teaspoon shah zeera (black cummin seeds)
2 teaspoons cummin powder
¼ teaspoon ground cloves
1 teaspoon ginger powder
1 teaspoon ground cinnamon
½ teaspoon black pepper
1 teaspoon chilli powder
salt to taste
100 g/4 oz ghee
300–450 ml/½–¾ pint yogurt

Wash and truss the chicken. Slice onions finely. Grind the garlic, poppy seeds, cardamoms and shah zeera to a paste. Add all the other spices to the paste with a little water. Rub the chicken with the paste after adding salt.

Heat the ghee in a heavy saucepan and fry the onions to golden brown. Remove crisp onions and keep aside. In the same fat fry the chicken with all the paste. Beat the yogurt till smooth and add the fried onions.

Pour this over the chicken, bring to the boil, then simmer covered till the chicken is tender. Uncover and fry for a few minutes till the liquid is absorbed. Serve with roti.

SPICED CHICKEN COOKED IN YOGURT

METRIC/IMPERIAL

1 (1.25-kg/2½-lb) chicken
1 large onion
3 cloves garlic
1 teaspoon ginger powder
50 g/2 oz cooking fat
1 teaspoon salt
450 ml/¾ pint yogurt
bunch coriander or watercress leaves
¼ green pepper, sliced
½ teaspoon turmeric
1 teaspoon garam masala

Wash and joint the chicken. Slice the onion finely. Grind the garlic to a paste and mix with the ginger powder.

Heat the fat and brown the onion. Add the garlic and ginger paste and salt and cook for 5 minutes. Add the chicken pieces and brown well. Add 900 ml/1½ pints hot water and simmer till the chicken is tender and about 4 tablespoons gravy remain.

Add the yogurt and the coriander or watercress leaves, the sliced green pepper, turmeric and garam masala and stir thoroughly. Bring to the boil and serve at once.

CHICKEN AND TOMATOES

METRIC/IMPERIAL

1 large onion
3 cloves garlic
½ teaspoon sugar
1 tablespoon vinegar
50 g/2 oz cooking fat or ghee
½ teaspoon ginger powder
1 (1.25-kg/2½-lb) chicken
675 g/1½ lb tomatoes
2 teaspoons garam masala
salt to taste

Slice the onion and garlic finely. Dissolve the sugar in the vinegar.

Heat the fat and fry the onions, garlic and ginger for 5 minutes. Add the chicken, jointed, and fry till browned, stirring so that the pieces do not stick to the pan. Add 2 litres/3½ pints hot water and simmer till the chicken is tender and just 300 ml/½ pint gravy remains.

Now add the halved tomatoes and simmer till half the liquid is absorbed. Add the garam masala, salt and vinegar mixture. Bring to the boil and cook for 3 minutes more. Serve hot.

CHICKEN CURRY (1)

METRIC/IMPERIAL

1 boiling chicken, jointed
2 onions, sliced
100 g/4 oz cooking fat
½ teaspoon turmeric
½ teaspoon cummin powder
½ teaspoon chilli powder
3 cloves garlic, mashed
600 ml/1 pint coconut milk
150 ml/¼ pint tamarind water
2 teaspoons salt

Boil the chicken and reserve the stock. Fry the onions in the fat till light brown. Add the mixed spices and fry. Add the chicken and mix well. Then add the coconut milk, tamarind water, salt and stock and simmer until the fat rises to the top.

The total cooking time will be approximately 2 hours.

CHICKEN CURRY (2)

METRIC/IMPERIAL

2 large onions
4 cloves garlic
1 teaspoon turmeric
1 teaspoon ginger powder
2 teaspoons coriander powder
1 teaspoon cummin powder
1 teaspoon chilli powder
1 teaspoon paprika
1 (1.25-kg/2½-lb) chicken
100 g/4 oz butter or ghee
2 bay leaves
1 small stick cinnamon
1 large cardamom
salt to taste
150 ml/¼ pint yogurt

Slice 1 onion finely. Grind the other onion with the garlic to make a paste. Add to this paste the turmeric, ginger, coriander, cummin, chilli and paprika. Cut the chicken into pieces.

Heat the ghee and fry the sliced onion till golden brown. Lower heat, add the bay leaves, cinnamon and the cardamom and fry for 1 minute.

Add the paste, chicken and salt and fry for 3 minutes. Beat the yogurt and add to the curry.

Bring to the boil and simmer very gently till almost cooked. Remove lid and fry till a rich brown colour and the chicken is tender.

If the chicken is not tender enough a little hot water may be added while cooking.

CHICKEN CURRY (3)

METRIC/IMPERIAL

1 (1.25-kg/2½-lb) chicken
2 onions
1 tomato
3 cloves garlic
50 g/2 oz cooking fat
1 teaspoon ginger powder
1 teaspoon turmeric
2 teaspoons coriander powder
1 teaspoon cummin seeds
¼ teaspoon chilli powder
2 teaspoons salt
300 ml/½ pint yogurt

Wash and joint the chicken. Slice onions and tomato. Chop garlic finely.

Heat the fat and fry the onions till brown. Add the garlic and ginger and fry the pieces of chicken with it till nicely browned. Stir all the time to prevent burning.

Now add the other spices and the salt. Fry for 2 minutes, then add the yogurt and 600 ml/1 pint hot water and simmer gently until chicken is cooked.

CHICKEN CURRY (4)

METRIC/IMPERIAL

50 g/2 oz cooking fat
2 large onions
2 bay leaves
½ teaspoon garam masala
2 cloves garlic, sliced finely
1 (1.25-kg/2½-lb) chicken
1 teaspoon salt
½ teaspoon sugar
¼ green pepper, sliced
½ teaspoon ginger powder
½ teaspoon cummin powder
¼ teaspoon chilli powder
1 pint thick coconut milk (see page 17)
3 large potatoes

Heat the fat. Slice 1 onion and chop the other. Fry the sliced onion and put in bay leaves and the garam masala. Put in the chopped onion, sliced garlic and washed and jointed chicken pieces and fry, stirring, till brown. Add the salt, sugar, sliced green pepper, ginger, cummin and chilli and fry another 5 minutes. Now add the coconut milk and simmer till chicken is done.

Then put in the pieces of potato (peeled, quartered and lightly fried) and simmer till chicken is soft. Add more hot water if cooking a tough bird, because the chicken must be very soft.

CHICKEN MILK CURRY

METRIC/IMPERIAL

1 (1.25-kg/2½-lb) chicken
75 g/3 oz onions
100 g/4 oz butter
1 teaspoon ginger powder
1 teaspoon curry powder
1 teaspoon poppy seeds
2 teaspoons black pepper
½ teaspoon chilli powder
25 g/1 oz desiccated coconut
2 teaspoons salt
50 g/2 oz ground almonds
600 ml/1 pint milk
juice of 3 lemons

Joint the chicken. Slice the onions finely. Heat the butter and fry the onions to a light cream colour. Add the ginger and fry till the onions are pale gold. Add the chicken to the onions and fry well.

Meanwhile add all the spices, coconut, salt and almonds to the milk and mix thoroughly. When the chicken has been well browned add the milk and spice mixture, cover and simmer gently. Stir occasionally, so as not to let the mixture stick to the pan.

When quite dry, if the chicken is not tender add spoonfuls of hot water and continue cooking. If a little gravy is required, add extra hot milk, and when curry is thick add the lemon juice. The juice should be heated before adding to the curry. Simmer till the fat floats on top then serve.

CHICKEN CURRY FROM THE SOUTH

METRIC/IMPERIAL

10 dried red chillies
2 tablespoons poppy seeds
2 tablespoons coriander seeds
½ teaspoon cummin seeds
6 cashew nuts
2.5-cm/1-inch piece fresh ginger or ½ teaspoon ginger powder
1 teaspoon turmeric
1 (1-kg/2-lb) chicken
1 fresh coconut
75 g/3 oz ghee
4 small onions
4 cloves garlic
salt to taste
juice of 1 lemon

Grind the chillies, poppy seeds, coriander, cummin, cashew nuts and fresh ginger if used to a paste and mix in the turmeric. Cut the chicken into pieces. Grate the coconut; drain out the coconut milk and reserve. Pour 600 ml/1 pint hot water over the coconut and let it soak.

Heat the ghee and fry the peeled onions, sliced garlic, ginger powder if used, paste, chicken and salt till they are brown. Squeeze the juice from the coconut and pour over the chicken. Simmer over low heat till the chicken is tender. Just before serving, add the thick coconut milk and the lemon juice.

LUCKNOW SPICED CHICKEN

Oven temperature: Moderately hot
190°C, 375°F, Gas Mark 5

METRIC/IMPERIAL

1 (1.5-kg/3-lb) chicken
5 large or 10 small tomatoes
1 large onion
6 cloves garlic
1 teaspoon turmeric
1 teaspoon cummin powder
1 teaspoon garam masala
½ teaspoon ginger powder
1 teaspoon salt
1 teaspoon castor sugar
50 g/2 oz cooking fat

Wash, clean and joint the chicken and pierce well with a fork. Skin and chop the tomatoes. Mince the onion and garlic and add to the turmeric, cummin, garam masala, ginger, salt and sugar. Rub the mixture well into the chicken and let the pieces marinate in the spices for at least 2 hours.

Then heat the fat in an enamel casserole and put in the chicken pieces with the spices and the tomatoes. Cover and put in the oven till chicken is soft and tender. Then transfer to top of stove, uncover, and fry on gentle heat till the spices and gravy are dry. Stir often so that chicken pieces do not stick to pan or burn.

BOMBAY CHICKEN CURRY

METRIC/IMPERIAL

1 (1.75-kg/4-lb) chicken, jointed
2 tablespoons vinegar
100 g/4 oz desiccated coconut
4 cloves garlic
½ teaspoon cummin powder
½ teaspoon turmeric
1 teaspoon chilli powder
½ teaspoon freshly ground pepper
2 tablespoons olive oil
1 teaspoon ginger powder
10 curry leaves
2 teaspoons salt
1 tablespoon sugar

Boil the chicken (in a pressure cooker if possible) and reserve the stock. Mix or grind together the vinegar, coconut, garlic, cummin, turmeric, chilli and pepper.

Heat the oil in a saucepan and gently fry all the mixed spices. Add the ginger and curry leaves and fry for 2 minutes. Add the chicken pieces and 300 ml/½ pint stock. Simmer for 15 minutes, then add the salt and sugar and remove from the heat after stirring.

This can be eaten hot or cold.

CHICKEN ALMOND CURRY
(Extravagant)

METRIC/IMPERIAL

1 (1.5-kg/3-lb) chicken
225 g/8 oz fresh coconut, grated
25 g/1 oz tamarind
4 large onions
8 cloves garlic
½ teaspoon ginger powder
350 g/12 oz butter or cooking fat
101 almonds
2 tablespoons desiccated coconut
1 teaspoon chilli powder
3 teaspoons cummin powder
3 teaspoons poppy seeds
1 tablespoon coriander seeds
2 pinches of saffron strands
salt to taste

Joint the chicken. Soak coconut in 300 ml/½ pint hot water for 10 minutes, then squeeze and strain the milk. Soak the tamarind in 150 ml/¼ pint water and squeeze and strain out the water after 10 minutes. Reserve the coconut milk and the tamarind water. Slice the onions finely. Crush or grind the garlic and mix with the ginger powder. Rub this into the chicken pieces and leave for 1 hour.

Heat 50 g/2 oz fat in a large pan. Fry the onions a light brown, add the chicken and fry till well browned. Add 1 litre/1¾ pints hot water and simmer till 150 ml/¼ pint of liquid remains and the chicken is tender.

Blanch the almonds. Grind or chop the almonds, desiccated coconut, chilli, cummin, poppy seeds and coriander. Add a little coconut milk if required.

In a clean pan heat the rest of the fat and cook the spices till they start to bubble. Mix this in with the chicken and bring to the boil twice. Mix the saffron with 2 tablespoons coconut milk. Add the remaining coconut milk to the curry with salt. Add the tamarind water and boil 3 times. Add the saffron mixed with the coconut milk and bring to the boil twice. Remove from the heat.

Serve with plain boiled rice. The curry will be thick and to taste its best the spices and almonds must be ground. 101 almonds must be counted and used. It is sometimes known as the 101-almond curry.

SPICED GRILLED CHICKEN

METRIC/IMPERIAL

1 (1.5–1.75-kg/3½–4-lb) chicken
½ teaspoon meat tenderizer
½ teaspoon garlic
½ teaspoon ginger powder
½ teaspoon chilli powder
¼ teaspoon curry powder
pinch of pepper
¼ teaspoon turmeric
1 teaspoon salt
25 g/1 oz cooking fat or butter
1 lemon, sliced

Clean, wash and joint the chicken and prick all over with a fork. Mix all the other ingredients except the fat, rub well into the forked chicken pieces and marinate for 2 hours.

Then brush all over with melted fat and grill under fierce grill at first to seal the juices in, and then gently until chicken is cooked and tender. Serve hot with lemon slices.

CHICKEN COOKED IN BREAD

Oven temperature: Moderate
160°C, 325°F, Gas Mark 3

METRIC/IMPERIAL

1 (1.5-kg/3-lb) chicken
1 small onion
7 cloves garlic
1¾ teaspoons ginger powder
2 teaspoons salt
250 g/9 oz cooking fat
7 large slices bread
2 tablespoons sugar
150 ml/¼ pint milk
¼ green pepper
4 teaspoons green coriander or watercress leaves
2 large onions
½ teaspoon turmeric
½ teaspoon chilli powder
½ teaspoon pepper
2 teaspoons Worcestershire sauce

Cut the chicken into pieces. Slice the small onion. Pound 4 cloves of garlic to a paste and add ginger and salt.

Heat 25 g/1 oz fat and fry the sliced onion and garlic paste till brown. Add chicken and brown well. Add 600 ml/1 pint hot water and salt and simmer till chicken is tender and 300 ml/½ pint gravy remains.

Cut each slice of bread lengthwise into 3 pieces. Dissolve the sugar in the milk and soak the bread in it for 10 minutes. Drain the pieces.

Heat 100 g/4 oz fat and fry the bread pieces golden brown. Drain and keep hot. Add any milk left over to the hot fat and reduce to form a thick sauce. Remove from heat and keep hot.

Chop remaining 3 cloves garlic, green pepper and coriander leaves. Slice or chop the 2 large onions and fry them golden brown in the remaining 100 g/4 oz fat. Add the turmeric, chopped garlic, green pepper, coriander, chilli and pepper and fry till brown. Remove and keep hot.

Mix the chicken gravy with the milk sauce and Worcestershire sauce.

Line a saucepan with half the drained bread slices. Put in the chicken pieces. Pour the fried chopped vegetables over the chicken and cover with rest of bread slices. Pour the gravy over.

Cover the pan and simmer over low heat for 5 minutes, then put into the oven for 30 minutes. Serve hot.

CHICKEN FARCHA
(Cutlets)

METRIC/IMPERIAL

1 chicken
3 cloves garlic
½ green pepper, chopped
2 teaspoons salt
2 teaspoons ginger powder
3 eggs
breadcrumbs
fat for deep frying

Cut chicken into 7 pieces, i.e. the 2 wings, the breast and 2 pieces from each leg. Scrape the meat carefully from the bone. Put in muslin cloth and flatten with a meat tenderizer. Grind or mash the garlic and green pepper together. Add the salt and ginger and apply the mixture to both sides of the cutlets. Keep aside for 5–6 hours (overnight if possible).

When ready to cook the cutlets, beat eggs lightly and dip the cutlets into them, then into breadcrumbs, and deep fry.

CHICKEN KORMA

METRIC/IMPERIAL

1 (1.25-kg/2½-lb) chicken
2 large onions
2 cloves garlic
1 teaspoon ginger powder
100 g/4 oz ghee
150 ml/¼ pint yogurt
1 teaspoon chilli powder (optional)
salt to taste
½ teaspoon cummin powder (kashmiri if available)
2 green cardamoms

Cut the chicken into joints. Slice the onions finely. Grind the garlic to a paste and mix with the ginger powder.

Heat the ghee and fry the onions a golden brown. Take out and keep aside.

Lower the heat and in the hot ghee fry the garlic paste, adding a little water. Add the chicken, yogurt, fried onions, chilli if used and salt and mix thoroughly. Cover and simmer till the chicken is nearly done. Add the kashmiri cummin. Grind the cardamoms coarsely and add to the curry. Fry for another 5 minutes and serve.

CHICKEN AND CAULIFLOWER POTATO STEW

METRIC/IMPERIAL

1 (1.5-kg/3½-lb) chicken
3 large potatoes
1 onion
25 g/1 oz cooking fat
½ teaspoon chilli powder
½ teaspoon ginger powder
3 cloves garlic
1 teaspoon salt
1 cauliflower
300 ml/½ pint thick coconut milk (see page 17)

Wash, clean and joint the chicken. Boil and quarter the potatoes, slice the onion, heat the fat. Add the sliced onions and fry to a cream colour. Put in the spices and the crushed garlic. Fry till spices no longer smell raw.

Add the pieces of chicken and brown well, turning continually to prevent burning. Add 900 ml/1½ pints warm water and salt and simmer.

When chicken is half cooked, add cauliflower broken into florets and coconut milk. After 10 minutes add the potatoes, and when the cauliflower is done and about 150 ml/¼ pint gravy remains, remove and serve hot.

GRILLED SPRING CHICKEN A LA BHAROOCH

METRIC/IMPERIAL

3 spring chickens
1 teaspoon chilli powder
1 teaspoon dry mustard
¼ teaspoon garlic salt
1 teaspoon turmeric
pinch of ginger powder
pinch of salt
1 tablespoon Worcestershire sauce
20 g/¾ oz butter

Roast the 3 spring chickens. When ready split them in halves. Mix the chilli, mustard, garlic salt, turmeric, ginger and salt with the Worcestershire sauce. Then bit by bit mix in the butter till it all resembles a paste. Smear the paste over the chicken halves and marinate for 3–4 hours, at least.

When desired, grill under medium grill for 10 minutes.

Serve hot with fried potatoes, peas and tossed salad.

Note: A large (1.5–1.75-kg/3½–4-lb) roasting chicken can be used instead of spring chickens, in which case roast first then joint into 2 legs, 2 wings and breast. Proceed as for spring chickens.

APRICOT CHICKEN

METRIC/IMPERIAL

1 (1.5-kg/3-lb) chicken
2 medium onions
2 medium tomatoes
2 cloves garlic
½ teaspoon ginger powder
¼ teaspoon chilli powder
¼ teaspoon saffron strands
1 tablespoon hot milk
2 tablespoons cooking fat
¼ teaspoon garam masala
2 teaspoons salt
225 g/8 oz apricots, stoned

Wash, clean and joint the chicken. Chop the onions finely. Blanch, skin and chop the tomatoes coarsely. Pound garlic into a paste with the ginger and chilli. Crumple the saffron into the hot milk and let it dissolve.

In a saucepan heat the fat and fry the onions a light cream colour. Put in the garlic, ginger and chilli paste and fry with the onions 5 minutes, stirring often. Now add the chicken pieces, garam masala, tomatoes and salt to the pan. Pour in 900 ml/1½ pints warm water and simmer gently until chicken is cooked and tender.

Remove cover occasionally to see that water has not evaporated. If it has, add a little warm water. When chicken is tender and done, add the saffron milk and stoned apricots and cook gently until apricots are soft and tender but not mushy.

Serve hot.

Note: Duck or any other poultry can be cooked like this with peaches or apricots. Tinned fruit can be used, but not the syrup.

COCONUT CHICKEN STEW

METRIC/IMPERIAL

1 (1.25-kg/2½-lb) chicken
5 onions
3 cloves garlic
½ green pepper
2 tablespoons coriander or watercress leaves
50 g/2 oz cooking fat
½ teaspoon garam masala
½ teaspoon ginger powder
3 teaspoons coriander powder
15 g/½ oz desiccated coconut
4 teaspoons poppy seeds
2 teaspoons salt
coconut milk (see page 17)
juice of 1 lemon
30 cashew nuts, fried

Wash, clean and joint the chicken. Peel and slice the onions finely. Crush the garlic. Slice the pepper into fine strips. Chop the coriander or watercress leaves well.

Heat the cooking fat in a saucepan and fry the sliced onions a light cream colour. Add the garam masala, crushed garlic, ginger, coriander, desiccated coconut, poppy seeds, salt, chopped coriander or watercress leaves and green pepper strips and fry for 10 minutes.

Put in the chicken pieces and fry until brown, stirring often so that chicken and spices do not burn. Now add 150 ml/¼ pint warm water and the coconut milk to the chicken. Cover tightly and simmer gently until chicken is soft and cooked. Add the lemon juice and cashew nuts. Stir well so that all is well mixed together.

Remove from heat and serve hot.

PARSEE CHICKEN CURRY

METRIC/IMPERIAL

1 boiling chicken
4 large onions
2 large tomatoes
2 red chillies
3 cloves garlic
100 g/4 oz cooking fat
1 teaspoon salt (minimum)
2 teaspoons cummin powder
2 teaspoons turmeric
½ teaspoon ground cinnamon
¼ teaspoon black pepper
¼ teaspoon ground cloves
¼ teaspoon ginger powder
150 ml/¼ pint yogurt
150 ml/¼ pint coconut milk (see page 17)

Cut the chicken in pieces and chop the onions, tomatoes, chillies and garlic. Fry the onions in the fat until they are creamy in colour and not browned. Add all the vegetables, salt and spices at intervals of 5 minutes between each one, mixing them in and frying with the onions.

Add the chicken, yogurt and coconut milk.

Cook on a low heat until the chicken is tender. It should take about 2 hours.

CHICKEN LIVERS AND GIZZARDS

METRIC/IMPERIAL

450 g/1 lb chicken livers and gizzards
225 g/8 oz onions
3 cloves garlic
100 g/4 oz butter or cooking fat
½ teaspoon ginger powder
1 teaspoon chilli powder
1 teaspoon salt

Clean the chicken livers and gizzards and cut each gizzard in half. Keep the gizzards separate from the livers. Slice the onions. Mash the garlic.

Heat the butter and in it fry the sliced onions a deep brown colour. Add the ginger and garlic and fry for another 7 minutes. Then add the chicken gizzards, chilli and salt and fry another 3 minutes. Add 600 ml/1 pint warm water to the gizzards and simmer partly covered till gizzards are soft and almost cooked. Lastly add the chicken livers and allow all to cook over very gentle heat.

Cover the saucepan completely and shake from time to time to prevent anything sticking. When gizzards and livers are soft and cooked, remove from heat and serve.

CHICKEN IMPERIAL

METRIC/IMPERIAL

1 (1.25-kg/2½-lb) chicken	25 g/1 oz cooking fat
3 medium onions	½ teaspoon ginger powder
½ green pepper or 2 green chillies	½ teaspoon black pepper
	1 teaspoon salt

Joint the chicken. Slice the onions and pepper or chillies.

Heat the fat and fry the onions until brown and crisp. Drain and reserve. Fry the chicken pieces in the hot fat over a medium heat. Turn constantly to avoid chicken pieces burning or sticking to the pan. When chicken pieces are half cooked, add ginger, green pepper, black pepper, salt and 150 ml/¼ pint warm water. Cover and simmer till chicken is tender.

Serve hot with the fried onions sprinkled on top.

OVEN-COOKED CHICKEN

Oven temperature: Moderately hot
190°C, 375°F, Gas Mark 5

METRIC/IMPERIAL

1 (1.5-kg/3-lb) chicken	1 teaspoon Worcestershire sauce
4 cloves garlic	1 teaspoon ginger powder
3 teaspoons lemon juice	1 tablespoon olive oil
1 teaspoon melted butter	¼ teaspoon chilli powder
2 tablespoons yogurt	1 teaspoon salt
½ teaspoon sugar	½ teaspoon turmeric

Keep the chicken whole but remove all skin. Mash the cloves of garlic and then chop finely. Mix the garlic and all the rest of the ingredients well. Prick the chicken very well, then rub the mixture into it. Let it marinate in the mixture for 24 hours in the refrigerator.

Then roast the chicken in the oven. Continually turn and baste the chicken until it is tender and cooked. Add hot water or fat while cooking as required.

PIGEON CURRY

METRIC/IMPERIAL

2 pigeons
100 g/4 oz freshly grated coconut
3 cloves garlic
4 medium onions
50 g/2 oz butter
6 curry leaves
1 teaspoon turmeric
2 teaspoons cummin powder
1 teaspoon ginger powder
2 teaspoons coriander powder
½ teaspoon chilli powder
½ teaspoon ground cinnamon
4 cloves
1 teaspoon salt
small bunch coriander or watercress leaves
2 teaspoons desiccated coconut
4 medium potatoes, chopped
juice of ½ lemon

Quarter the pigeons. Soak the fresh coconut in 150 ml/¼ pint hot water and extract the milk after 10 minutes. Chop the garlic and slice the onions finely.

Heat the fat and fry half the onions with the curry leaves till golden brown. Add the turmeric and fry for 1 minute then add tablespoons of hot water from time to time while cooking the onions until they are quite soft.

Add the cummin and fry for 3 minutes then add 2 teaspoons water. Add the other spices and salt one by one, frying for 3 minutes and adding 2 teaspoons of water and stirring after each one. Then add the salt, the rest of the onions, garlic, coriander leaves and pigeon quarters.

Fry for 5 minutes in the sauce then add the desiccated coconut, coconut milk and 150 ml/¼ pint hot water. Cover and simmer for 30 minutes.

When the pigeon is half cooked add the chopped potatoes with 4 tablespoons hot water. Cook for 20 minutes, then add lemon juice and simmer for 5 minutes.

CHICKEN KABAB

Oven temperature: Moderately hot
190°C, 375°F, Gas Mark 5

METRIC/IMPERIAL

2 medium onions
3 cloves garlic
4 cloves
4 peppercorns
150 ml/¼ pint yogurt
½ teaspoon ginger powder
1 teaspoon chilli powder
½ tablespoon vinegar
salt to taste
1 (1.25-kg/2½-lb) chicken
butter for basting

Grind the onions, garlic, cloves and peppercorns to a paste. Put the yogurt in a large bowl and mix in the paste, spices, vinegar and salt. Prick the cleaned chicken with a fork and rub in the yogurt mixture. Leave the chicken to marinate in the bowl for 1–2 hours.

Cook on a rotary spit and baste with butter. If you do not have a spit, roast the chicken in the usual way in the oven. Baste with butter. This kabab is generally eaten with chapatis or parathas and a salad of sliced onions in lemon juice.

TANDOORI CHICKEN

Oven temperature: Moderately hot
190°C, 375°F, Gas Mark 5

METRIC/IMPERIAL

1 (1-kg/2-lb) roasting chicken
1 large onion, chopped
4 cloves garlic
2.5-cm/1-inch piece fresh ginger or ½ teaspoon ginger powder
1 teaspoon coriander powder
1 teaspoon cummin powder
½ teaspoon chilli powder
2 teaspoons salt
150 ml/¼ pint yogurt
1 tablespoon vinegar
1 tablespoon Worcestershire sauce
2 lemons
25 g/1 oz melted butter
1 teaspoon garam masala

Clean the chicken, keep whole but do not truss. Make 3–4 cuts on each side of the bird. Grind the onion, garlic and ginger to a paste; add to it the coriander, cummin, chilli and salt. Beat the yogurt in a bowl and add the paste, vinegar, Worcestershire sauce and the juice of 1 lemon. Mix thoroughly and rub over the chicken. Marinate the chicken for 4–5 hours.

Roast in the oven for 20 minutes or till the chicken is tender. If possible cook on a barbecue rotary spit. Brush with melted butter, sprinkle over garam masala and more lemon juice and serve.

Note: Tandoori chicken is cooked in a special kind of oven. The word 'Tandoor' means oven. A large, long earthenware pot is embedded in clay and earth. Charcoal is put inside and the oven is made red hot. The chicken or meat is put inside on skewers. The meats cooked in these ovens taste superb; no other can give the same delicious flavour, but this is a close approximation.

CHICKEN MULLIGATAWNY (1)

METRIC/IMPERIAL

- 100 g/4 oz fresh coconut or 50 g/2 oz desiccated coconut
- 2 medium onions
- 100 g/4 oz cooking fat
- 4 teaspoons poppy seeds
- 2 tablespoons coriander powder
- 2 teaspoons gram flour
- 1 (1.25-kg/2½-lb) chicken
- 1 teaspoon salt
- ¼ teaspoon chilli powder
- 12 almonds or 50 g/2 oz ground almonds
- 1 lemon, sliced

Grate the fresh coconut and soak in 150 ml/¼ pint hot water for 10 minutes; squeeze and strain the milk. Slice the onions finely and fry in 25 g/1 oz fat till golden brown. Remove and crush. Grind the poppy seeds to a paste and mix in the coriander, gram flour and onions. Joint the chicken and put in a pan with water to just cover and salt. Bring to the boil and simmer till the chicken is tender. Remove the chicken pieces and set aside. Reserve the stock.

In a clean saucepan, heat 75 g/3 oz fat and add the paste, chilli, almonds and the coconut milk. Add the chicken stock and when the mixture gets thick add the chicken pieces. Allow to come to the boil and simmer for 3 minutes.

Serve with plain boiled rice and lemon slices.

CHICKEN MULLIGATAWNY (2)

METRIC/IMPERIAL

10 peppercorns
½ teaspoon ginger powder
2 teaspoons turmeric
1 tablespoon coriander powder
1 teaspoon chilli powder
1 onion
1 small boiling chicken
2 tablespoons ghee or butter
salt to taste
1 lemon, sliced

Grind the peppercorns and mix with all the powdered spices. Moisten them with a little water to make a paste. Slice the onion finely. Joint the chicken and simmer in a generous litre/2 pints water. After 10 minutes add the paste and simmer on till the chicken pieces are tender. Strain the soup.

Heat the ghee in a clean pan and fry the onion till golden brown. Add to this the soup and chicken pieces. Season with salt and bring to the boil once. Serve with boiled rice and lemon slices.

CHICKEN VINDALOO

METRIC/IMPERIAL

1 (1.5-kg/3-lb) chicken
1 teaspoon mustard seeds
6 cloves garlic
2 large onions
2 teaspoons turmeric
1 teaspoon ginger powder
1 stick cinnamon
2 teaspoons chilli powder
2 teaspoons cummin powder
6 cloves
2½ tablespoons vinegar
1 tablespoon brown sugar
salt to taste
75 g/3 oz ghee

Wash and dry the chicken; cut into pieces. Grind the mustard seeds. Grind the garlic and 1 onion to a paste. Slice the other onion. Put the chicken in a bowl with the mustard, garlic paste and all the other spices and the vinegar, sugar and salt and marinate for 4 hours.

Heat the ghee, fry the onion slices then add the chicken and all the paste and simmer till the chicken is tender. The saucepan must be covered with a tight-fitting lid while simmering.

ROAST DUCK WITH SPICES

Oven temperature: Moderate
180°C, 350°F, Gas Mark 4

METRIC/IMPERIAL

2 large onions	½ teaspoon ginger powder
2 green chillies	salt to taste
1 small duck	½ teaspoon garam masala
4 thick slices bread	½ teaspoon turmeric
milk	1 teaspoon black pepper
225 g/8 oz mashed potatoes	50 g/2 oz ghee or butter

Chop the onions, chillies and duck giblets. Remove the crusts from the bread and soak the slices in milk. Squeeze out the milk then mix together the potatoes, bread, ginger and the chopped ingredients. Add salt and garam masala and mix well. Stuff the duck with this mixture.

Make a paste with the turmeric, pepper, more salt and a little water and rub over the duck.

Melt the ghee and pour over the duck. Roast it in an uncovered pan, allowing 20–30 minutes per half kilo/pound. Baste with its own juices.

CURRIED DUCK (1)

METRIC/IMPERIAL

1 large duck	¼ teaspoon ginger powder
¼ green pepper	½ teaspoon black pepper
6 cloves garlic	4 tablespoons vinegar
¼ teaspoon chilli powder	4 tablespoons olive oil
½ teaspoon cummin powder	2 teaspoons salt
½ teaspoon turmeric	½ teaspoon sugar

Cut the duck into pieces. Wash and dry. Chop the green pepper very finely. Crush the cloves of garlic. Mix the chilli, cummin, turmeric, ginger, pepper, garlic and chopped green pepper with the vinegar. Rub the pieces of duck with this paste, and marinate for at least 3 hours.

Heat the oil. Put in the pieces of duck, add the salt and cook with the pan covered over a very low heat. Add 2 tablespoons water if duck sticks to saucepan.

Just before removing from the heat add the sugar.

CURRIED DUCK (2)

METRIC/IMPERIAL

- 1 large onion
- 3 tablespoons coriander seeds
- 1 teaspoon cummin seeds
- ½ teaspoon fenugreek seeds
- 1 teaspoon poppy seeds
- 4 cloves garlic
- 2.5-cm/1-inch piece green ginger
- 1½ teaspoons turmeric
- ½ fresh coconut
- 1 small duck
- 75 g/3 oz ghee
- 1 teaspoon chilli powder
- salt to taste
- juice of 1 lemon

Slice the onion. In a dry frying pan roast the coriander, cummin, fenugreek and poppy seeds. Do not let them burn. Grind the garlic, ginger and the roasted spices and add the turmeric to the paste. Grate the coconut and soak it in 300 ml/½ pint boiling water for 1 hour. Squeeze out the milk. Strain.

Joint the duck. Fry the onion in the ghee and when golden brown add the paste and fry over a low heat for 3 minutes. Add the duck and fry for another 3 minutes. Cover and cook for 5 minutes over gentle heat then add 300 ml/½ pint warm water, chilli powder and salt and simmer till duck is tender.

Add the coconut milk and lemon juice 10 minutes before serving. Serve with rice.

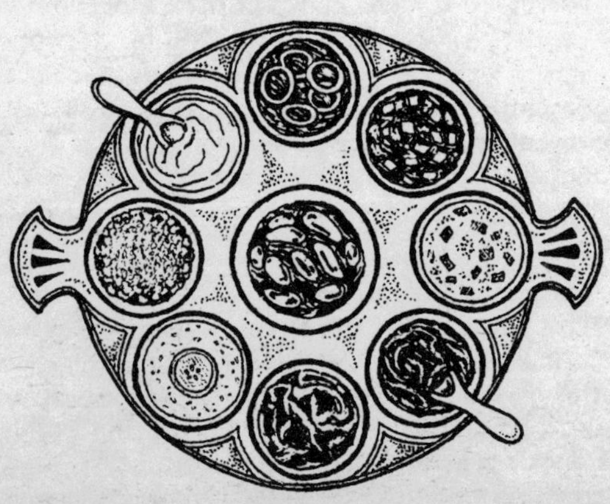

Fish

India has a large variety of fish, both salt and freshwater. Fish figure largely in the diet of coastal areas in the west and east, but particularly in the latter region, because of the great rivers that flow through Bengal to the sea. Bengalis eat fish at every meal, and one of the best known curries is called Macher Jhol. Pomfret and ravas — the Indian salmon — are popular on the Bombay coast and, of course, there is the well-known Bombay Duck, a slim herring size fish, for which Europeans seem to have acquired more of a taste than most Indians.

The medium most used for cooking fish in India is oil, especially mustard oil, which has a higher burning point than butter.

To remove the muddy taste and the smell of freshwater fish, gram flour is usually rubbed on the fish, which is then left for 30 minutes or so then washed thoroughly.

BENGALI FISH CURRY (1)
(Macher Jhol)

METRIC/IMPERIAL

450 g/1 lb fish cutlets
1 teaspoon mustard seeds
1 medium onion
3 green chillies
3 tablespoons mustard or other cooking oil
salt to taste
½ teaspoon turmeric

Wash and dry the fish. Grind the mustard seeds into a paste. Chop onion and green chillies.

Heat the oil and fry the fish on both sides. Add onion, chillies and salt. Fry for 3 minutes. Mix the mustard paste and turmeric in 300 ml/½ pint water and add to the fish.

Cook till fish is tender.

BENGALI FISH CURRY (2)

METRIC/IMPERIAL

450 g/1 lb white fish
2 tomatoes
3 cloves garlic
150 ml/¼ pint tamarind water (see page 18)
1 teaspoon ginger powder
¼ teaspoon chilli powder
½ teaspoon turmeric
300 ml/½ pint yogurt
2 tablespoons mustard or other cooking oil
½ teaspoon fenugreek seeds
2 teaspoons salt
½ bunch fresh coriander or watercress leaves
juice of 1 lemon

Clean and cut fish into pieces. Slice tomatoes. Mash the garlic cloves and mix in the tamarind water. Add the ginger and mix well. Set aside. Put the fish in a bowl and add the chilli, turmeric and yogurt. Set aside for 30 minutes.

Heat the oil. Put in fenugreek seeds and fry until brown. Add the contents of the bowl, salt and the coriander leaves. Simmer gently for at least 10 minutes. Now add the spiced tamarind water and the tomatoes. Simmer until the tomatoes are done (about 5 minutes). Add the lemon juice and serve with rice.

FISH KOFTA CURRY

METRIC/IMPERIAL

1 kg/2 lb white fish
3 medium onions
salt to taste
1 bay leaf
2 green chillies
a few sprigs of coriander or parsley
1 egg
2 tablespoons soft breadcrumbs
225 g/8 oz ghee
1 clove garlic
1 teaspoon coriander powder
½ teaspoon cummin powder
1 teaspoon turmeric
1 teaspoon chilli powder
½ teaspoon ginger powder
225 g/8 oz tomatoes, chopped

Cook the fish in a little water with ½ peeled onion, salt and the bay leaf till tender. Remove and cool but keep the strained liquid.

Chop the green chillies and coriander leaves. Mash the fish and mix with the chopped chillies and coriander leaves, egg and breadcrumbs. Shape into balls the size of a plum and fry in ghee till brown. Drain and keep aside.

Slice 1 onion finely. Grind the rest of the onions and the garlic to a paste and add all the other spices.

Reheat the ghee and fry the sliced onion golden brown. Add the spice paste and fry over low heat for 5 minutes. Add the chopped tomatoes and more salt and cook covered till tomatoes are mixed in the gravy. Add the liquid from the fish and 300 ml/½ pint water and bring to the boil; put in the fish balls and simmer for 10 minutes.

Drain and serve with rice.

FISH CURRY WITH THICK GRAVY

METRIC/IMPERIAL

1 kg/2 lb fish steaks
1 large onion
½ green pepper or 2 green chillies
1 bunch coriander leaves or 1 teaspoon coriander powder
2 cloves garlic
15 g/½ oz tamarind pulp
2 teaspoons gram flour
½ teaspoon sugar
50 g/2 oz cooking fat or oil
½ teaspoon curry powder
1 teaspoon salt

Wash fish. Chop the onion finely. Chop the green pepper or chillies and the coriander leaves. Chop the garlic. Soak the tamarind pulp in 150 ml/¼ pint water, squeeze and strain juice.

In a dry frying pan roast the gram flour. Keep the heat low and stir till the gram flour smells cooked. Mix the sugar with the tamarind juice.

Heat the fat and fry the onion light golden. Add the curry powder, garlic, green pepper and coriander leaves. Fry over low heat for 10 minutes, then add gram flour and keep stirring. Then add the tamarind juice, salt and fish. Mix. Cover and simmer till fish is cooked and the gravy is thick.

FISH CURRY WITH YOGURT

METRIC/IMPERIAL

1 kg/2 lb firm-fleshed fish
150 ml/¼ pint yogurt
450 g/1 lb onions
¼ teaspoon ginger powder
4 tablespoons oil or cooking fat
1 teaspoon turmeric
salt to taste
1 teaspoon mixed ground cardamoms, cloves and cinnamon

Wash and cut fish into steaks and marinate them in half the yogurt for 30 minutes. Slice half the onions finely and grind the rest to a paste. Mix the ginger powder with the onion paste. Beat the remaining yogurt till smooth.

Heat the fat and fry the sliced onions till golden brown. Add the ginger and onion paste, turmeric and salt and fry over low heat for 2–3 minutes.

Add the fish, yogurt and remaining ingredients and cook till the fish is tender.

PRAWN MALLAI CURRY

METRIC/IMPERIAL

225 g/8 oz freshly grated coconut
450 g/1 lb prawns
2 onions
½ teaspoon ginger powder
½ teaspoon turmeric
½ teaspoon garam masala
50 g/2 oz ghee
salt to taste
1 teaspoon sugar
1 tablespoon treacle

Steep the coconut in 300 ml/½ pint hot water. Squeeze and strain. Clean the prawns and remove the black thread. Wash and drain them. Slice 1 onion finely. Grind the other onion to a paste and add to it the ginger, turmeric and garam masala.

Heat the fat and fry the prawns. Remove and keep aside. In the same fat fry the sliced onions till golden brown. Add the onion and spice paste, salt and sugar and fry till the paste is nicely browned. Add the prawns and the coconut milk. Cook till prawns are tender.

Add the treacle and serve.

CRAB CURRY

METRIC/IMPERIAL

2 large crabs or 2 (198-g/7-oz) tins crabmeat
4 cloves garlic
1 teaspoon ginger powder
2 onions
50 g/2 oz cooking fat
300 ml/½ pint yogurt
½ teaspoon turmeric
¼ teaspoon chilli powder
3 cloves
1 tablespoon watercress leaves
1 teaspoon salt

Boil and dress crabs. Mash garlic in 150 ml/¼ pint water and add the ginger to it. Slice onions.

Heat the fat and fry onions till brown. Add the crabmeat, yogurt, turmeric, chilli, cloves and watercress leaves. Simmer for 10 minutes, then add the salt and garlic water. Simmer another 5 minutes and serve.

GOA PRAWN CURRY

METRIC/IMPERIAL

2 tablespoons desiccated coconut
9 dried red chillies
8 cloves garlic
4 teaspoons coriander seeds
20 fenugreek seeds
1 teaspoon cummin seeds
1 teaspoon salt
¼ teaspoon dry mustard
½ teaspoon turmeric
½ teaspoon ginger powder
1 teaspoon garam masala
1 onion, chopped
50 g/2 oz butter
600 ml/1 pint thick coconut milk (see page 17)
4 tablespoons tamarind water (see page 18)
4–5 dozen cooked prawns
1 onion, sliced
1 teaspoon paprika

Soak desiccated coconut in 2 tablespoons hot water. Mince it very finely with the red chillies and garlic. Grind the coriander, fenugreek and cummin seeds and mix into the coconut with the salt, mustard, turmeric, ginger and garam masala. Set aside.

Fry the chopped onion to a light cream colour in the heated butter. Add the coconut and garlic mixture, stir well and fry till it smells. Add the coconut milk and tamarind water. Simmer for 5 minutes and put in the prawns, sliced onion and paprika. Stir well. Cook gently till the juice is thick.

PRAWN CURRY

METRIC/IMPERIAL

4 cloves garlic
1 teaspoon ginger powder
1 medium onion
50 g/2 oz cooking fat
2 teaspoons coriander powder
¼ teaspoon chilli powder
½ teaspoon cummin powder
1 teaspoon turmeric
300 ml/½ pint yogurt
1 teaspoon salt
225 g/8 oz cooked prawns or shrimps

Mash garlic and add with ginger to 150 ml/¼ pint water and set aside. Dice onion.

Heat the fat and fry the onion till brown. Add the powdered spices, yogurt, garlic and ginger water and salt. Simmer for 10 minutes.

Add the prawns and simmer until they are heated through.

SOUR FISH

Oven temperature: Hot
220°C, 425°F, Gas Mark 7

METRIC/IMPERIAL

¼ green pepper
2 tablespoons fresh coriander or watercress leaves
3 cloves garlic
2 teaspoons gram flour
¼ teaspoon turmeric
⅛ teaspoon chilli powder
¼ teaspoon cummin powder
¾ teaspoon salt
4 tablespoons vinegar
1 tablespoon melted cooking fat
4 white fish fillets

Chop green pepper and coriander leaves very finely. Mash garlic cloves. Mix gram flour, green pepper, coriander leaves, garlic, powdered spices, salt and vinegar well together, and stir into the melted fat. Rub this mixture over the pieces of fish.

Wrap and seal each piece of fish in foil. Put into a baking tin and place in the oven. Bake for 10–15 minutes till fish is soft.

STEAMED FISH

METRIC/IMPERIAL

450 g/1 lb white fish
15 g/½ oz almonds
2 bay leaves
½ green pepper, chopped
2 teaspoons salt
15 g/½ oz mustard oil
300 ml/½ pint yogurt
½ teaspoon garam masala
½ teaspoon sugar

Clean and slice fish. Blanch and toast almonds. Mix the other ingredients together with the almonds, put on the fish slices and steam the mixture in a covered pan or steamer until fish is done.

BENGALI PRAWN CURRY

METRIC/IMPERIAL

1 egg
225 g/8 oz prawns
2 teaspoons coriander seeds
1 large onion
2 teaspoons parsley
breadcrumbs
2 tablespoons mustard oil
¼ teaspoon chilli powder
½ teaspoon garlic salt
½ teaspoon ginger powder
3 bay leaves
salt to taste
juice of ½ lemon

Beat the egg. Boil the prawns. Crush coriander seeds. Slice onion finely. Chop parsley. Mince prawns and mix with coriander seeds and parsley. Make into balls the size of walnuts. Dip in egg, then into breadcrumbs. Cover and set aside.

Heat the oil and fry onion until brown. Add spices, bay leaves and salt and fry 5 minutes. Add 150 ml/¼ pint hot water and prawn balls. Simmer 10 minutes.

Add lemon juice. Shake pan and serve.

PARSEE PRAWN CURRY

METRIC/IMPERIAL

2 teaspoons brown sugar
300 ml/½ pint tamarind water (see page 18)
2 tablespoons sweet cooking oil
5 onions, sliced finely
225 g/8 oz cooked prawns
1 teaspoon salt
2 teaspoons chopped coriander or watercress leaves
½ teaspoon cummin seeds
3 cloves garlic, chopped finely
½ teaspoon turmeric

Dissolve sugar in tamarind water. Heat the oil to very hot in a frying pan and put in the onions, prawns and salt. Cover and simmer for a few minutes, stirring occasionally.

Put in the chopped coriander leaves and spices. Stir and simmer for 10 minutes. Pour in tamarind and sugar water.

Simmer till all the moisture has evaporated.

BENGALI CRAB KOFTA CURRY

METRIC/IMPERIAL

2 crabs or 2 (198-g/7-oz) cans crabmeat
1 large onion
1 teaspoon parsley
1 egg
¼ teaspoon chilli powder
½ teaspoon black pepper
4 cloves garlic, crushed
2 teaspoons coriander seeds
breadcrumbs
2 tablespoons mustard oil
4 bay leaves
2 teaspoons salt
juice of ½ lemon

Boil and dress crabs. Slice the onion and chop the parsley. Beat the egg with a fork. Mix chilli, pepper and crushed garlic. Pound the crabmeat and coriander seeds together. Mix the parsley, garlic and crabmeat mixtures and make into balls the size of walnuts. Dip balls into beaten egg and roll in breadcrumbs.

Heat the oil and fry the sliced onion till brown. Add bay leaves and salt and fry for 5 minutes.

Add 150 ml/¼ pint hot water and the fish balls. Simmer for 10 minutes then add lemon juice. Shake the pan and remove from the heat.

LOBSTER CURRY

METRIC/IMPERIAL

1 large lobster
4 cloves garlic
50 g/2 oz cooking fat
2 onions, sliced
300 ml/½ pint yogurt
½ teaspoon turmeric
¼ teaspoon chilli powder
3 cloves
1 tablespoon watercress leaves
1 teaspoon salt
1 teaspoon ginger powder

Boil the lobster in its shell then remove meat and cut in pieces. Mash garlic in 150 ml/¼ pint water.

Heat the fat and fry the onion in it till browned. Add the pieces of lobster, yogurt, turmeric, chilli, cloves and watercress leaves. Simmer gently for 10 minutes. Sprinkle with salt. Add the ginger and garlic water. Simmer 5 minutes more. Remove and serve hot.

BENGALI LOBSTER BALL CURRY

METRIC/IMPERIAL

1 large lobster, boiled
2 teaspoons coriander seeds
1 egg, beaten
breadcrumbs
50 g/2 oz mustard oil
1 large onion, sliced
¼ teaspoon chilli powder
½ teaspoon ginger powder
3 bay leaves
½ teaspoon garlic salt
1 teaspoon salt
juice of ½ lemon

Remove and mince the lobstermeat and crush the coriander seeds. Mix together and make into balls. Dip first into beaten egg then into breadcrumbs. Put aside.

Heat the mustard oil and fry the sliced onion in it till brown. Add the spices, bay leaves, garlic salt and salt and fry for 5 minutes. Now add the fish balls and 150 ml/¼ pint hot water, and simmer for 10 minutes. Add the lemon juice. Shake the pan and remove from heat.

DRY BOMBAY DUCK AND SPINACH CURRY

METRIC/IMPERIAL

225 g/8 oz onions
12 dried Bombay ducks
675 g/1½ lb spinach
7 cloves garlic
2 bunches coriander or watercress leaves
½ green pepper
50 g/2 oz sweet or frying oil
¾ teaspoon cummin seeds
½ teaspoon tumeric
1 teaspoon salt
¼ teaspoon chilli powder

Chop the onions finely. Cut Bombay ducks into 3–4 pieces each, or use any other dried fish cut into 2.5-cm/1-inch cubes. Wash the spinach, drain and chop. Chop finely the garlic, coriander or watercress leaves and the green pepper.

Fry the onions in the heated oil and add the chopped garlic, coriander or watercress leaves and the green pepper, and the cummin, turmeric, salt and spinach. When spinach is half cooked add the chilli and stir. Add the fish and let it simmer till all is soft and no trace of liquid remains.

BOMBAY DUCK OR DRIED FISH CURRY (1)

METRIC/IMPERIAL

4 cloves garlic
bunch of coriander or watercress leaves
½ green pepper
3 large onions
1 teaspoon sugar
1 tablespoon Worcestershire sauce
25 g/1 oz butter
1 tablespoon olive oil
12 dried Bombay ducks

Chop the garlic finely. Chop the coriander leaves and green pepper finely. Chop the onions coarsely. Mix the sugar with the Worcestershire sauce. Mix the butter and olive oil. Soak the fish in hot water for 30 minutes then drain thoroughly, remove the bones and shred the fish.

Heat the fat in a pan and fry the onions till light cream in colour. Add all the chopped ingredients and the fish and stir till everything is well mixed. Cover pan and simmer gently till the fish is tender. Pour in the Worcestershire sauce mixture just before removing from the heat. Stir and serve.

BOMBAY DUCK CURRY (2)

METRIC/IMPERIAL

25 g/1 oz tamarind
6 dried Bombay ducks
4 cloves garlic
1 medium onion
50 g/2 oz cooking fat
½ teaspoon turmeric
½ teaspoon black pepper
¼ teaspoon chilli powder
¼ teaspoon ginger powder
few sprigs of coriander or watercress

Soak the tamarind in 150 ml/¼ pint water for 10 minutes or more, then squeeze and strain the juice. Cut the fish into 3.5-cm/1½-inch pieces. Mash the garlic and slice the onions finely.

Heat the fat and fry the onions a pale cream colour. Add the turmeric, garlic, pepper, chilli, ginger and the coriander sprigs. Fry till the spices and onions are lightly browned then add the tamarind juice.

Bring to the boil and add the fish. Cover and simmer gently till the fish is tender.

CURRIED HERRINGS

METRIC/IMPERIAL

2 medium onions
2 cloves garlic
1 tablespoon tamarind pulp
4 herrings
1½ teaspoons coriander powder
½ teaspoon ginger powder
1 teaspoon garam masala
1 teaspoon turmeric
1 teaspoon cummin powder
2 teaspoons chilli powder
salt to taste
75 g/3 oz ghee or oil

Slice onions finely. Chop the garlic. Soak the tarmarind in 600 ml/1 pint water and squeeze out the juice. Strain.

Wash, clean and cut the fish into steaks. Put in a bowl and pour the tamarind water over the fish. Add all the spices, salt and garlic and leave for 15 minutes.

Heat the ghee and fry the onions golden brown; add the fish with all the spice mixture and liquid. Bring to the boil then simmer covered for 20 minutes.

CURRIED PILCHARDS

METRIC/IMPERIAL

2 onions
1 clove garlic
1 teaspoon coriander powder
½ teaspoon cummin powder
¼ teaspoon ginger powder
1 teaspoon turmeric
1 teaspoon chilli powder
2 tomatoes
50 g/2 oz ghee
1 (454-g/1-lb) can pilchards
2 green chillies, chopped
salt to taste
1 teaspoon garam masala

Slice 1 onion finely. Grind the other onion and the garlic to a paste. Add all the powdered spices except the garam masala to the garlic paste with a little water to keep it moist. Chop the tomatoes.

Heat the ghee and fry the onion slices till brown; add the paste and fry over low heat for 5 minutes. Add the tomatoes, cover and cook for another 5 minutes. Add the drained fish, chopped chillies and salt. Cover and simmer till fish is heated through. Sprinkle with garam masala and serve.

PARSEE DRY BEAN AND ROE CURRY

METRIC/IMPERIAL

2 onions, sliced
3 tablespoons sweet oil
1 clove garlic
⅛ teaspoon ginger powder
⅛ teaspoon chilli powder
½ teaspoon turmeric
¼ teaspoon cummin powder
1 teaspoon salt
1 tablespoon coriander leaves, chopped
300 ml/½ pint coconut milk (see page 17)
350 g/12 oz frozen beans
2 teaspoons sugar
300 ml/½ pint tamarind water (see page 18)
225 g/8 oz fresh cod's roe

Fry the sliced onions in 1½ tablespoons sweet oil until light cream colour. Mash the garlic with the ginger and chilli to make a paste and add to the onions. Stir and fry 2 minutes. Then add the turmeric, cummin, salt and chopped leaves. Fry for 2 minutes, and pour in the coconut milk. Add the beans after the coconut milk has come to the boil. Dissolve the sugar in the tamarind water and add to the pan.

Fry the pieces of roe in the rest of the sweet oil and add to the beans when most of the moisture has evaporated.

When the oil comes to the top, remove from heat.

SHRIMP AND MARROW STEW

METRIC/IMPERIAL

450 g/1 lb marrow
225 g/8 oz shrimps or prawns
½ green pepper
40 g/1½ oz cooking fat
½ teaspoon cummin powder
1 bay leaf
½ teaspoon turmeric
½ teaspoon coriander powder
¼ teaspoon chilli powder
1 teaspoon salt
2 teaspoons milk
½ teaspoon sugar

Peel, steam and cut the marrow into small cubes. Clean and boil shrimps. Slice green pepper.

Heat fat and fry the cummin, bay leaf and green pepper until soft. Add the turmeric, coriander and chilli and cook till spices start to smell. Add the marrow, shrimps, salt, milk and sugar. Simmer for 5 minutes.

DAHI MACH
(Fish in Yogurt)

METRIC/IMPERIAL

1 kg/2 lb firm-fleshed fish
2 teaspoons turmeric
salt to taste
2 onions
1 teaspoon ginger powder or small piece fresh ginger
3 green chillies
450 ml/¾ pint yogurt
1 teaspoon chilli powder
50 g/2 oz mustard oil
50 g/2 oz ghee
2 teaspoons garam masala

Wash and cut the fish into fair size pieces. Make a paste with turmeric, salt and water and rub on the fish. Slice 1 onion. Grind the other onion and ginger to a paste. Slice the green chillies. Beat the yogurt and add the fish, onion paste, green chillies and chilli powder and leave to soak for 30 minutes.

Heat the oil and ghee in a saucepan. Fry the sliced onion till lightly browned then add the fish mixture and the garam masala.

Bring to the boil and simmer very slowly, covered, till the fish is cooked. There should be a rich and thick gravy.

Serve with boiled rice.

FISH AND VEGETABLE STEW (1)

METRIC/IMPERIAL

- 2 onions
- 1 large aubergine
- 450 g/1 lb cod
- 1 teaspoon turmeric
- 1½ teaspoons salt
- 1 tablespoon mustard oil
- ¼ teaspoon fenugreek seeds
- ¼ teaspoon cummin seeds
- ¼ teaspoon mustard seeds
- 2 bay leaves
- 1 red chilli
- 100 g/4 oz peas
- ½ marrow, sliced
- 3 potatoes, diced
- ½ teaspoon sugar

Slice 1 onion thinly and chop the other finely. Slice aubergine in rounds. Skin the cod and cut in 4 pieces. Rub with ¼ teaspoon turmeric and ½ teaspoon salt. Leave for 30 minutes, then fry in a little mustard oil.

Heat the rest of the oil and fry the spice seeds for 1 minute. Put in bay leaves, sliced onion and red chilli. Fry another minute. Now add the remaining turmeric, vegetables and fish, and fry for 5 minutes. Put in the chopped onion, remaining salt, sugar and 300 ml/½ pint hot water. Simmer covered until vegetables are cooked and the slightly disintegrated fish has made the gravy thick.

A soup can be made by adding a little more hot water. Serve with fried croûtons.

FISH AND VEGETABLE STEW (2)

METRIC/IMPERIAL

2 onions
¼ green pepper
3 large potatoes
225 g/8 oz peas
1 cauliflower
450 g/1 lb white fish
2 teaspoons salt
¾ teaspoon turmeric
4 tablespoons mustard oil
½ teaspoon garam masala
¼ teaspoon chilli powder
¼ teaspoon ginger powder
1 teaspoon sugar
150 ml/¼ pint yogurt

Slice 1 onion thinly and chop the other finely. Slice green pepper thinly. Boil potatoes and cube. Boil peas. Boil cauliflower and cut in large pieces. Clean and cut fish into 12 pieces. Rub in 1 teaspoon salt and ¼ teaspoon turmeric. Fry in 2 tablespoons of the mustard oil.

Heat the rest of the oil well. Fry the garam masala for 3 minutes, add the sliced onion and fry to a light cream colour. Now put in the chopped onion, the chilli, ginger and remaining turmeric. Fry gently for 5 minutes, stirring often. Put in the remaining salt, the sugar, a little hot water, vegetables, fish and yogurt.

Simmer very gently till fish is cooked.

FISH PATIA

METRIC/IMPERIAL

1 plaice
4 cloves garlic
25 g/1 oz tamarind
4 teaspoons gram flour
2 tablespoons oil
50 g/2 oz cooking fat
½ teaspoon chilli powder
½ teaspoon cummin powder
½ teaspoon turmeric
1 teaspoon salt
sugar (optional)

Wash and cut the fish into slices. Chop the garlic finely. Soak the tamarind in 150 ml/¼ pint water for 10 minutes, then squeeze and strain the juice. Roast the gram flour in a dry frying pan or in the oven till the flour is a shade darker.

Heat the oil and fat and fry the garlic, chilli, cummin and turmeric till they begin to smell cooked and are a reddish colour. Add the gram flour and 450 ml/¾ pint hot water and stir.

When the curry begins to thicken add the fish. Simmer till the fish is almost ready, then add the tamarind water and salt. A little sugar may be added if liked.

Simmer gently for 15 minutes and serve with rice.

TARAPOREE PATIA

METRIC/IMPERIAL

15–20 dried Bombay ducks or other dried fish	1 teaspoon chilli powder
4 cloves garlic	½ teaspoon salt
½ teaspoon cummin powder	6 tablespoons vinegar
½ teaspoon turmeric	1½ tablespoons sweet oil
	2 teaspoons brown sugar

Cut the dried fish into pieces. Crush the garlic and mix with all the spices and salt. Add a little vinegar to make into a paste.

Heat the oil and put in the spice paste. Cook till the raw smell of the spices disappears, then add the fish and cook till it is almost tender.

Dissolve the sugar in the remaining vinegar and add to fish. Simmer gently till fish is quite cooked and the liquid nearly gone.

Note: This curry is a speciality of a town called Tarapore.

FISH KABABS

METRIC/IMPERIAL

1 kg/2 lb firm-fleshed fish	½ teaspoon ginger powder
2 cloves garlic	1 teaspoon chilli powder
100 g/4 oz onions	2 teaspoons garam masala
150 ml/¼ pint yogurt	melted butter for basting
salt to taste	

Cut the fish into cubes. Grind the garlic and add it to the bowl of water in which the fish is to be washed. Wash and drain the fish cubes. Grind the onions and mix with the yogurt, salt and spices. Marinate the fish in the yogurt mixture for 2 hours.

Thread the fish on to skewers and grill until cooked through, turning often. Brush with melted butter while grilling.

PRAWN CUTLETS

METRIC/IMPERIAL

8 large prawns
2 medium onions
½ teaspoon ginger powder
½ teaspoon chilli powder
salt to taste
1 large egg, beaten
breadcrumbs
fat for frying

Remove shells from prawns but keep the tails. Slit the prawns down the back and remove the black thread. Wash and dry them and place on a board. Flatten and slit the prawns lightly all over.

Grind the onions to a paste and add the ginger, chilli and salt. Rub this paste over the flattened prawns, then dip them in beaten egg and coat with breadcrumbs.

Fry in shallow fat until tender and crisp. Drain and serve warm.

PRAWN KOFTAS

METRIC/IMPERIAL

225 g/8 oz cooked prawns
1 onion
¼ teaspoon sugar
2 teaspoons vinegar
½ bunch coriander or watercress leaves
½ green pepper
3 cloves garlic
¼ teaspoon turmeric
2 teaspoons gram flour
¼ teaspoon chilli powder
1 teaspoon salt
100 g/4 oz cooking fat

Mince the prawns. Chop onion finely. Mix sugar and vinegar. Chop coriander leaves, green pepper and garlic. Mix onion with prawns in a bowl. Add all other ingredients except fat and mix well by hand.

Make into walnut size balls and fry in very hot cooking fat till reddish brown. The koftas must be cooked through. If necessary, fry gently afterwards for a few minutes in a frying pan.

SPICY POTATO CAKES
(With Fish Stuffing)

METRIC/IMPERIAL

4 large potatoes
450 g/1 lb fish fillets
2 onions
1 clove garlic
½ teaspoon ginger powder
vegetable oil or fat for frying
1 teaspoon chilli powder
salt to taste
1 teaspoon garam masala
1 egg, beaten
breadcrumbs

Boil and mash the potatoes. Steam the fish in a steamer or pan with a tight-fitting lid. Mash it with a fork. Chop 1 onion finely. Grind the other onion and garlic to a paste; add ginger.

Heat 25 g/1 oz fat and fry the chopped onion till lightly browned; add the onion paste and chilli and fry for 2 minutes. Add the fish, salt and garam masala and fry for 5–6 minutes; remove from the heat. Cool.

Add salt to mashed poatoes and shape into round or oval cakes. Put some fish in the middle and cover with potato mixture. Dip in beaten egg, roll in breadcrumbs and fry in shallow hot fat until brown. Drain and serve warm.

GREEN PEPPERS STUFFED WITH PRAWNS

Oven temperature: Hot
220°C, 425°F, Gas Mark 7

METRIC/IMPERIAL

4 large green peppers
5 cloves garlic
3 large onions
15 g/½ oz cooking fat
¼ teaspoon ginger powder
¼ teaspoon chilli powder
½ teaspoon paprika
1 teaspoon salt
½ teaspoon cummin powder
¼ teaspoon turmeric
3 (92-g/3¼-oz) cans peeled prawns

Cut the green peppers in half. Take out the seeds and the knob of flesh near the top. Scald in hot water and set aside. Chop the garlic and the onions very finely.

Heat the cooking fat in a frying pan and fry the garlic, ginger, chilli, paprika, salt, cummin and turmeric for 5 minutes. Then add the prawns and onions, stirring the mixture now and again so that it does not burn. Turn the heat low and cover pan. Simmer until shrimps are soft. Stuff the mixture into the prepared green peppers.

Place the peppers carefully in a greased ovenproof dish. Place the dish in a roasting pan containing hot water. Cook in the oven for 30 minutes.

ROASTED SPICED FISH

Oven temperature: Moderate
180°C, 350°F, Gas Mark 4

METRIC/IMPERIAL

¼ green pepper
bunch coriander leaves or parsley
1 teaspoon cummin powder
¼ teaspoon chilli powder
½ teaspoon ginger powder
½ teaspoon garlic salt
1 tablespoon garlic vinegar
1 (450-g–1-kg/1–2-lb) whole fish
25 g/1 oz butter
flour (optional)

Chop the green pepper and coriander leaves. Mix them with the spices and garlic salt into the vinegar. Stuff the cleaned fish with the mixture but rub some on the fish as well. Butter the fish and tie with string or wrap in foil. Put in greased baking dish and bake in the oven.

If baked unwrapped, baste with butter and turn when red. When fish is cooked pour off the gravy and thicken with a little flour, or leave the gravy as it is if preferred.

SPICED GRILLED FISH

METRIC/IMPERIAL

450 g/1 lb fish steaks or or 1 whole fish
bunch coriander or watercress leaves
¼ green pepper
salt
¼ teaspoon garlic salt
juice of ½ lemon
25 g/1 oz butter
1 lemon, sliced

If whole fish is used have it cleaned and prepared for stuffing. Chop the coriander leaves and green pepper very finely. Rub fish with salt. Heat the grill to medium strength. Mix the chopped leaves, green pepper, garlic salt and lemon juice. Rub the fish steaks with this mixture or stuff the fish with it. Dot with butter and grill.

When one side is done, turn and dot the second side with butter. When fish is cooked remove to a hot dish. Pour the gravy from the bottom of the pan over the fish.

Serve with boiled potatoes and lemon slices.

COCONUT SPICED FISH

METRIC/IMPERIAL

450 g/1 lb white fish
3 tablespoons mustard oil
3 onions, chopped
½ green pepper, chopped
300 ml/½ pint thick coconut milk (see page 17)
2 teaspoons salt
juice of 1 lemon

Cut the fish across in slices and fry in part of the mustard oil. In the rest of the heated mustard oil fry the chopped onions and green pepper until the onions are a deep cream colour. Add the fish, coconut milk and salt. Cover and simmer till fish is cooked.

Remove from heat and add the lemon juice. Shake saucepan to mix.

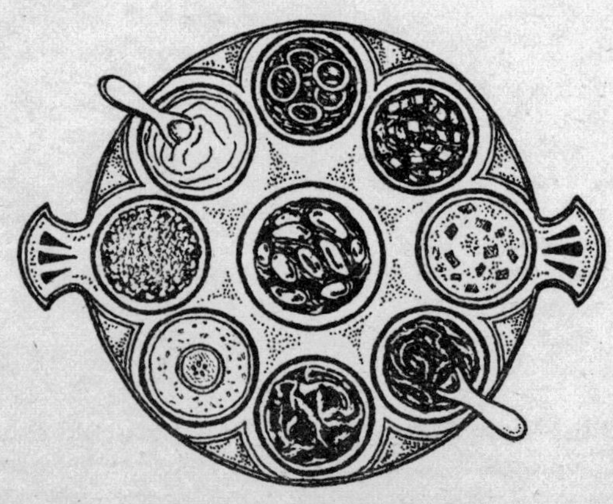

Eggs

Eggs form part of the diet of most vegetarians as well as non-vegetarians in India (though there are some orthodox vegetarians who do not eat them).

Eggs can be cooked in very elaborate ways but they are also an excellent basis for quickly cooked, simple yet substantial dishes. As they can be stored easily they are a very good standby for when unexpected guests arrive.

EGG BHURJI
(Scrambled Eggs)

METRIC/IMPERIAL

- 2 medium onions
- 2 or more green chillies
- few coriander, mint or parsley leaves
- 4–5 large eggs
- salt to taste
- 50 g/2 oz butter

Slice the onions finely. Chop the chillies and the coriander leaves. Beat the eggs and add salt, chillies and coriander.

Heat the butter in a large frying pan and fry the onions till lightly browned. Add the eggs and stir with a fork till set. Do not overcook.

EGG CURRY SOUTH INDIAN STYLE

METRIC/IMPERIAL

- 1 large fresh coconut
- 2 large onions
- 2.5-cm/1-inch piece green ginger or 1 teaspoon ginger powder
- 2–3 green chillies
- 4 cloves garlic
- 4 tablespoons ghee or butter
- 1 teaspoon turmeric
- 1 tablespoon flour
- 300 ml/½ pint milk
- salt to taste
- juice of 2 lemons
- 1 tablespoon vinegar
- hard-boiled eggs

Grate the coconut and soak it in 300 ml/½ pint hot water for 10 minutes. Squeeze out the milk and strain. Reserve the milk. Add another 300 ml/½ pint hot water to the coconut pulp, squeeze and strain after 10 minutes. Keep this milk separate.

Slice the onions finely. Scrape and slice the green ginger if used into thin long strips. Slice the chillies and cut the garlic into very small pieces.

Heat the ghee and fry the onions and garlic a pale golden colour. Add the sliced chillies and ginger and fry till the chillies change colour. Add the turmeric, powdered ginger if used and flour and fry for a few seconds. Add the milk and the second 300 ml/½ pint of coconut milk. Simmer slowly till the gravy is reduced to half quantity. Add the first amount of coconut milk and salt to taste and simmer gently for 3 minutes. Add the lemon juice and the vinegar and put in the hard-boiled eggs, cut in half. Simmer gently for 10 minutes.

EGG CURRY (1)

METRIC/IMPERIAL

- 4–6 eggs
- 2 onions
- 2 cloves garlic
- 225 g/8 oz tomatoes
- 100 g/4 oz ghee or butter
- 1 teaspoon ginger powder
- 2 teaspoons coriander powder
- 1 teaspoon chilli powder
- 1 teaspoon garam masala
- 1 teaspoon turmeric
- 1 teaspoon cummin powder
- 1 teaspoon paprika
- salt to taste

Hard-boil the eggs and when cold cut in half. Slice 1 onion; grind the other onion and the garlic to a paste. Chop the tomatoes.

Heat the ghee and fry the sliced onion to a golden brown.

Take pan off the heat and add the paste, the other spices and salt.

Fry on a low heat for 5 minutes. Add the tomatoes, cover and simmer till the gravy is thick. Add the eggs and simmer for 5 minutes.

EGG CURRY (2)

METRIC/IMPERIAL

- 4 eggs
- 1 large onion
- 2 tomatoes
- 25 g/1 oz cooking fat
- 4 cloves garlic, mashed
- ½ teaspoon ginger powder
- 2 teaspoons salt
- ½ teaspoon chilli powder
- 1 teaspoon curry powder

Hard-boil the eggs, shell and halve when cool. Slice the onion and coarsely chop the tomatoes.

Heat the fat and fry the onions until cream colour. Add the garlic and ginger and fry for 3 more minutes. Then add the tomatoes, salt, chilli and curry powder and fry another 2 minutes, stirring all the time. Put in 300 ml/½ pint hot water and simmer till curry is thickened. Add the eggs. Simmer 5 minutes more and remove from heat.

BAKED SPICED EGGS

Oven temperature: Moderately hot
200°C, 400°F, Gas Mark 6

METRIC/IMPERIAL

2 large onions
2 cloves garlic (optional)
small bunch fresh coriander or watercress leaves
¼ green pepper
1 tablespoon vinegar or Worcestershire sauce
1 teaspoon sugar
50 g/2 oz cooking fat
4 eggs
½ teaspoon cummin powder
½ teaspoon salt

Thinly slice onions. Finely chop garlic if used, coriander leaves and green pepper. Mix the vinegar or Worcestershire sauce with the sugar.

Fry the onions in cooking fat till almond coloured. Add the garlic, green pepper and coriander to the onions. Fry for 3 minutes, stirring all the time. Beat the eggs and add to the onions in the saucepan. Add cummin powder. Remove from heat and pour in vinegar or Worcestershire sauce mixture and salt. Stir well.

Pour into an ovenproof dish and put in the oven to set. It should take just over 30 minutes to set.

SPICED DAL WITH EGGS

METRIC/IMPERIAL

4 eggs
6 large onions
2 bunches coriander or watercress leaves
¼ green pepper
225 g/8 oz mung dal
225 g/8 oz tuar dal
1 teaspoon turmeric
2 teaspoons salt
100 g/4 oz cooking fat
2 teaspoons cummin powder

Beat the eggs lightly and put aside. Slice 4 onions and chop the other 2. Finely chop the coriander leaves and green pepper.

Wash the two kinds of dal well. Put in a large saucepan and add the turmeric and salt. Cover with water and boil. When soft, mash well.

Fry the sliced onions until deep brown in the cooking fat. Add the chopped coriander, green pepper, cummin and chopped onions and cook for 3–5 minutes. Add the dal and mix well together. Remove from heat and cool.

When nearly cold, add the beaten eggs little by little, stirring all the time. Simmer on a very low heat for 5 minutes, stirring constantly. Be careful to keep the heat very low or the eggs will separate.

When ready to serve reheat very gently and carefully without bringing to the boil.

POACHED EGGS IN BATTER WITH CURRY SAUCE

METRIC/IMPERIAL

4 eggs
100 g/4 oz cooking fat

for batter:
1 egg
50 g/2 oz flour
50 g/2 oz softened butter

for sauce:
1 onion, chopped
2 teaspoons flour
15 g/½ oz butter
½ teaspoon cayenne
2 dashes Tabasco
2 teaspoons curry powder
1 teaspoon salt
300 ml/½ pint milk

To make batter, separate the egg and beat the white till stiff. Mix the yolk with the flour and butter, then fold into the stiffly beaten white. Poach the 4 eggs, dip them in the batter and fry crisp in the heated cooking fat. Remove the eggs and keep warm.

To make the sauce use the heated fat in which you fried the eggs to fry the chopped onion light brown. Add the flour and butter and cook till it starts to honeycomb. Now stir and add the cayenne pepper, Tabasco, curry powder and salt. Stir well. Add the milk slowly and simmer over very low heat till sauce thickens. Serve eggs and sauce with rice.

POTATO EGGS

METRIC/IMPERIAL

50 g/2 oz vinegar
2 teaspoons sugar
½ teaspoon chilli powder
450 g/1 lb potatoes
fat for frying
2 large onions
5 medium tomatoes, skinned and chopped
1 teaspoon salt
6 eggs

Mix the vinegar, sugar and chilli together. Wash, dry and cut potatoes into matchstick shapes, then fry till nearly crisp in deep fat. Remove chips and fry onions until pale cream colour. Then combine the two in a frying pan with 50 g/2 oz melted cooking fat.

Add the tomatoes and cook gently till soft. Add salt. Break the eggs carefully over the vegetables. Sprinkle all over with the vinegar mixture and simmer gently until eggs are set.

Note: They set more quickly if covered.

RICH PARSEE OMELETTE

METRIC/IMPERIAL

2 bunches coriander leaves
½ green pepper
6 cloves garlic
225 g/8 oz onions
¼ teaspoon sugar
50 g/2 oz tamarind water (see page 18)
12 eggs
1 teaspoon salt
2 teaspoons ginger powder
175 g/6 oz cooking fat

Chop the coriander leaves, green pepper, garlic and onions very finely. Mix the sugar into the tamarind water. Mix 6 whole eggs and the yolks of the other 6 in a bowl. Add all the ingredients except the onions and cooking fat. Stir till well blended.

Now fry onions to a cream colour in the fat in a deep frying pan and add the egg mixture, stirring meanwhile. Cook gently until the underside is done.

Then light the grill, put the frying pan under it and cook until top side is done. Keep scraping with a spatula to prevent it sticking to the pan.

When ready invert on a hot dish and cut into wedges.

EGGS AND POTTED SHRIMPS

METRIC/IMPERIAL

3 ripe bananas
2 large onions
½ green pepper
2 cloves garlic
7 g/¼ oz cooking fat
2 teaspoons olive oil
1 (125-g/4½-oz) jar potted shrimps
¼ teaspoon coriander powder
¼ teaspoon turmeric
¼ teaspoon cummin powder
salt to taste
4 teaspoons vinegar
1 tablespoon Worcestershire sauce
4 eggs, separated

Slice bananas in rounds. Slice onions thinly. Chop green pepper and garlic finely.

Heat cooking fat and fry the banana slices. In a heated frying pan heat the oil to very hot. Add the onion and shrimps and cover with lid. Turn the heat low and cook gently until onions are light cream in colour and the shrimps separated. Stir occasionally.

After 15 minutes add the chopped ingredients, the spices, salt, vinegar, Worcestershire sauce and fried banana slices. Stir gently, and cook on low heat. Beat the egg whites and add the yolks. Spread the shrimp mixture in the frying pan. Pour the eggs over it. Keep over low heat till eggs are set.

EGGS ON CAULIFLOWER

Oven temperature: Moderate
180°C, 350°C, Gas Mark 4

METRIC/IMPERIAL

2 cloves garlic
1 large onion
¼ green pepper
1 large cauliflower
40 g/1½ oz cooking fat
½ teaspoon coriander powder
½ teaspoon ginger powder
½ teaspoon turmeric
½ teaspoon cummin powder
1 teaspoon salt
4 eggs

Slice garlic, onions and green pepper finely. Boil cauliflower. Separate into florets and slice stems.

Heat the fat in a saucepan and fry the onions until creamy in colour. Add the cauliflower, garlic, onion, green pepper and the spices and salt. Stir well and simmer gently till everything is nearly a pulp.

Turn into a frying pan and make depressions with a spoon in the spiced vegetables. Break 1 egg in each depression. Simmer until eggs are set.

Note: Alternatively the cooked vegetables can be put into a greased ovenproof dish, and after the eggs are broken into the dish it should be put in the oven for the eggs to set, about 20–30 minutes.

CURRIED DUCK EGGS

METRIC/IMPERIAL

4 duck eggs
225 g/8 oz potatoes
2 medium onions
1-cm/½-inch piece fresh ginger or ¼ teaspoon ginger powder
2 cloves garlic
1 teaspoon turmeric
1 teaspoon chilli powder
2 green cardamoms
2 cloves
2.5-cm/1-inch stick cinnamon
75 g/3 oz ghee
2 tablespoons yogurt
salt to taste
1 teaspoon sugar

Hard-boil, then peel the eggs. When quite cold make slits all over them.

Peel the potatoes and, if large, cut into quarters. Slice 1 onion finely, grind the other onion with the ginger and garlic to a paste. Add to the paste the turmeric and chilli powder. Crush the cardamom seeds, cloves and cinnamon to a coarse powder.

Heat the ghee and fry the potatoes a pale gold. Drain and keep aside. In the same ghee brown the onions and fry the paste for 3–4 minutes. Add the potatoes, eggs, yogurt, salt and sugar with 150 ml/¼ pint warm water and simmer till there is a thick gravy. Sprinkle with the clove, cardamom and cinnamon powder.

BAKED EGGS AND MEAT

Oven temperature: Moderate
180°C, 350°F, Gas Mark 4

METRIC/IMPERIAL

450 g/1 lb meat
4 cloves garlic
1 teaspoon ginger powder
1 medium onion
25 g/1 oz melted butter or fat
1 teaspoon salt
5 eggs
½ teaspoon black pepper
breadcrumbs

Cut meat into pieces. Grind the garlic and mix in the ginger. Slice the onion finely.

Heat the fat and fry the onion till lightly browned. Add the garlic paste and salt and stir. Put in the meat and fry till the meat is dark brown. Add 600 ml/1 pint hot water. Simmer till the meat is tender and about 150 ml/¼ pint gravy remains. Remove from heat and cool.

Remove any bones and shred the meat. Break the eggs in a bowl, add pepper and beat lightly. Put the gravy and half the shredded meat in a greased ovenproof dish, and pour the eggs over the meat. Spread the rest of the meat over the eggs.

Cover with the breadcrumbs and bake in the oven till eggs are set and crumbs are browned.

STUFFED HARD-BOILED EGGS

METRIC/IMPERIAL

1 large onion
15 g/½ oz desiccated coconut
6 eggs
1 teaspoon curry powder
½ teaspoon garam masala
50 g/2 oz butter

Slice the onion. Soak coconut in 150 ml/¼ pint hot water. Hard-boil eggs. Shell when cool and cut in half. Remove yolks and mash together with the curry powder and garam masala, coconut and 25 g/1 oz butter. Stuff the whites with the mixture.

Heat the remaining butter and brown the onion. Put in 150 ml/¼ pint hot water and stuffed eggs. Bring to the boil, then simmer till liquid has evaporated.

PRESERVED EGGS

Boil 12 eggs quite hard and shell. Put in a large-mouthed jar with a layer of bay leaves between each layer of eggs. Use any of the following four ways to pickle the eggs. In all cases let the eggs change colour before using.

1. Boil enough malt vinegar to cover eggs, with 1 teaspoon each of peppercorns, small dried red chillies and sliced green ginger. When nearly cold pour all over eggs and cork the jar.
2. Boil the malt vinegar with 3 cloves, 1 bay leaf, a sprig each of thyme and parsley, 1 tablespoon brown sugar and 6 peppercorns. Pour over the eggs when cold and cork the jar.
3. Boil 25 g/1 oz chopped green ginger, 1 teaspoon cloves, a blade of mace and 1 teaspoon peppercorns in a generous litre/2 pints malt vinegar. Leave to steep for 3 days, then strain and pour the cold vinegar over the eggs. Cork the jar.
4. Simmer 25 g/1 oz black pepper, 25 g/1 oz ginger powder, 25 g/1 oz salt, 25 g/1 oz brown mustard seeds and 25 g/1 oz sliced onions in a generous litre/2 pints malt vinegar. Pour over eggs while hot. When cold cork the jar and tie down closely.

Pulses

Pulses, known as dal, are of many different varieties and are served at every meal. They can be cooked either in liquid form or fried dry and crisp.

Because pulses form a nourishing and filling dish and are cheaper than meat and vegetables, they form, with bread, the staple diet of the poor. The proverbial hospitality of the poorest Indian is summed up in the invitation, 'Please share my dal roti.'

DAL

METRIC/IMPERIAL

225 g/8 oz masoor, mung or chana dal
½ teaspoon turmeric
salt to taste
25 g/1 oz butter or ghee
1 medium onion, chopped finely
3–4 red chillies, chopped
½ teaspoon ginger powder

Wash the dal thoroughly in cold water. In a large saucepan put the dal, turmeric and 2.25 litres/4 pints water and bring to the boil. As the dal is liable to boil over, keep an eye on the pan and skim the froth. Lower the heat, add salt, cover the pan and simmer gently till the dal is soft. Stir well till the dal and water are well mixed and there is a smooth soup.

In a frying pan heat the fat and fry the chopped onion and chillies and add the ginger. Turn the contents of the frying pan into the dal very carefully as the fat splutters when poured into the liquid. Mix well before serving.

CHANA DAL

METRIC/IMPERIAL

225 g/8 oz chana dal
2 green chillies
1 medium onion
50 g/2 oz ghee
½ teaspoon turmeric
1 teaspoon cummin seeds
1 teaspoon mustard seeds
salt to taste
2 tablespoons freshly grated coconut
few sprigs of coriander (optional)

Wash and soak dal overnight. Drain and grind coarsely. Chop the green chillies. Chop the onion finely.

Heat the ghee and fry the onion till it is a pale gold. Add the turmeric, cummin and mustard seeds. When the mustard seeds begin to splutter and burst, add the ground dal and salt and fry. Cover and cook over low heat for 10 minutes. Add the coconut and green chillies, cover and cook for 5 minutes.

If liked add a few sprigs of coriander to the cooked dal.

DRY URAD DAL

METRIC/IMPERIAL

225 g/8 oz urad dal
1 medium onion
75 g/3 oz ghee or butter
½ teaspoon cummin seeds
1 teaspoon coriander powder
salt to taste
½ teaspoon ginger powder or small piece fresh ginger, sliced
½ teaspoon turmeric
1 teaspoon chilli powder

Wash dal and soak in cold water for 2–3 hours. Slice onion finely. Drain the dal.

Heat 50 g/2 oz of the fat and fry the cummin seeds. When the seeds rise to the surface add the dal and fry for a little while. Add coriander, salt, ginger, turmeric and chilli and fry for 4 minutes. Add enough water to come 2.5 cm/1 inch above the contents of the pan. Bring to the boil then simmer over very low heat till the dal is tender and all the water absorbed.

Heat 25 g/1 oz fat and fry the onions until golden brown. Turn the onions and fat carefully into the dal and serve.

KHATTI DAL
(Sour Dal)

METRIC/IMPERIAL

225 g/8 oz masoor, mung or arhar dal
½ teaspoon turmeric
salt to taste
½ teaspoon ginger powder
juice of 1 lemon
1 teaspoon sugar
2–3 green chillis, sliced (optional)
50 g/2 oz ghee or butter
½ teaspoon cummin seeds

Wash the dal and put in a pan with a generous litre/2 pints water, turmeric and salt. Bring to the boil and then simmer gently till the dal is tender. Mix thoroughly till the mixture is like thick soup. Add the ginger, lemon juice and the sugar and cook for 2–3 minutes. If liked add sliced green chillies to the dal.

In a frying pan heat the ghee, fry the cummin seeds and add to the dal.

DAL CUTLETS

METRIC/IMPERIAL

225 g/8 oz chana dal
1 teaspoon turmeric
¼ teaspoon ginger powder
1 medium onion
1–2 green chillies
coriander or mint leaves
salt and pepper
1 egg, beaten
breadcrumbs
fat for frying

Wash the dal and soak it in 300 ml/½ pint water for 1 hour. Boil the dal in the same water after adding the turmeric and ginger. If the water dries before the dal is soft add a little hot water. When quite soft and dry remove from the heat and grind to a paste.

Chop the onion, chillies and leaves. Add chopped ingredients, salt and pepper to the dal and shape into cutlets. Dip in egg and coat with crumbs. Fry till golden brown.

Leftover dal can also be used to make cutlets.

DAL AND POTATO STEW

METRIC/IMPERIAL

225 g/8 oz chana dal
2 onions
3 large tomatoes
2 large potatoes
¼ teaspoon ginger powder
75 g/3 oz cooking fat
¼ teaspoon chilli powder
2 teaspoons salt
¼ teaspoon turmeric
2 teaspoons garam masala
1 teaspoon sugar

Soak dal overnight in 150 ml/¼ pint hot water. Chop 1 onion finely. Extract the juice of the other (see page 18). Skin tomatoes. Peel and cut potatoes in cubes.

Boil dal in enough water to cover, and when it is soft, mash it in a mouli grinder. Mix ginger and onion juice into a paste.

Fry the potatoes in 25 g/1 oz fat till light brown in colour. Heat 15 g/½ oz fat and fry the ginger paste, the mashed dal, chilli and salt. Simmer till dry. Spread on a plate to cool, then cut into cubes.

Heat the rest of the fat and fry the chopped onion and remaining spices until onions are almond in colour. Add tomatoes, potatoes, sugar and 150 ml/¼ pint hot water. Simmer until potatoes are cooked. Add the cubes of dal and shake the pan so that the cubes mix with the other ingredients, but do not break. Simmer another 5 minutes.

DAHI BARA OR BHALLE

METRIC/IMPERIAL

- 225 g/8 oz urad dal
- 225 g/8 oz vegetable fat or ghee
- salt to taste
- 450 ml/¾ pint yogurt
- 1 teaspoon cummin seeds, roasted and ground
- 1 teaspoon garam masala
- 1 teaspoon chilli powder

Soak dal overnight. Drain, then grind in an electric grinder or on a grinding stone to a fine paste. Beat this paste till frothy. If too dry, add a little warm water.

Heat the fat in a deep frying pan. Take a cup and wet a small piece of muslin with water. Pull the muslin tightly over the open end of the cup; on this put a small piece of dal paste and pat into a small round cake. Make a hole in the centre and slip the cake into the hot fat. Make as many as you can out of the paste and fry golden brown over a medium heat. Drain.

Soak the fried baras in boiling salted water for 5 minutes then remove and squeeze the baras between your hands so that all the water is removed. Beat the yogurt and add the cummin and more salt. Put the baras in a serving dish and pour the yogurt over. Sprinkle with the garam masala and chilli.

DAL AND TOMATO STEW

METRIC/IMPERIAL

1 medium onion
3 cloves garlic
1 tablespoon coriander or watercress leaves
225 g/8 oz tomatoes
100 g/4 oz orange lentils
salt to taste
25 g/1 oz cooking fat
½ teaspoon ginger powder
¼ teaspoon chilli powder
¼ teaspoon turmeric
½ teaspoon cummin powder
⅛ teaspoon dry mustard
8 bay leaves

Chop onion, garlic and coriander leaves. Skin and quarter tomatoes. Boil lentils and tomatoes in a saucepan with water to cover, and add the chopped onion and salt. When lentils are soft, mash and strain through coarse sieve.

Heat fat in a saucepan. Mix the ginger, chilli, turmeric, cummin and mustard and fry gently for 5 minutes. Add the garlic, coriander and bay leaves. Add the lentil and tomato purée. Boil for 1 minute. Serve hot.

KABULI CHANA KHATTA
(Sour Spanish Peas)

METRIC/IMPERIAL

225 g/8 oz kabuli chana (Spanish chick peas)
1 medium onion
100 g/4 oz potatoes, boiled
50 g/2 oz tamarind
pinch of bicarbonate of soda
50 g/2 oz ghee or butter
1 teaspoon cummin seeds
1 teaspoon ginger powder
2 teaspoons chilli powder
salt to taste
2 teaspoons sugar
2 teaspoons garam masala

Wash peas and soak in plenty of water overnight. Slice onions finely. Dice potatoes. Soak tamarind in 300 ml/½ pint warm water.

Boil peas in a large saucepan with plenty of water and the bicarbonate of soda. Simmer till peas are tender. Strain the peas and reserve the stock.

Heat the fat and fry the onions a pale brown. Add the cummin seeds and fry for 2 minutes. Now put in the peas, ginger and chilli and fry. Add some of the stock and cook gently for 5 minutes. Add the potatoes and more stock and cook covered for a short time.

Squeeze the tamarind and strain the juice. Add the tamarind juice, salt and sugar and cook for another 5 minutes. Just before serving sprinkle with garam masala.

This is a Punjabi dish and is very delicious.

LOBIA DAL
(Black-eyed Bean Dal)

METRIC/IMPERIAL

225 g/8 oz lobia (black-eyed beans)	salt to taste
1 teaspoon turmeric	1 teaspoon chilli powder
1 teaspoon ginger powder	1 large onion
	50 g/2 oz ghee or butter

Boil 1.75 litres/3 pints water and put in the washed beans. Simmer until the beans are soft. Add the turmeric, ginger, salt and chilli. Slice onion finely.

Heat the fat in a frying pan and fry the onions a golden brown. Add this to the dal carefully before serving.

LOBIA CURRY
(Black-eyed Bean Curry)

METRIC/IMPERIAL

225 g/8 oz lobia	1 teaspoon chilli powder
50 g/2 oz ghee or butter	2 teaspoons coriander powder
1 large onion, sliced	salt to taste
1 teaspoon turmeric	3 tablespoons yogurt
1 teaspoon ginger powder	

Wash the lobia and put into a generous litre/2 pints boiling water. Bring to the boil and simmer till the beans are tender. Strain the beans and reserve the water.

In a saucepan heat the fat and fry the thinly sliced onion a golden brown. Add all the spices, salt and yogurt and fry for 5 minutes over a medium heat. Now add the lobia and fry for another 5 minutes; add 600 ml/1 pint of the water in which the lobia was boiled. If there is not enough water left over, then add enough water to make up the measured amount and simmer for 10 minutes.

Vegetables

Though vegetable dishes are included in meals all over India, they are the main diet of the many people who are strictly vegetarian because of religious principles. Therefore, like meat dishes, the preparation of vegetable dishes is highly developed, and varies from the simplest kinds to very elaborate ones.

As there are many Indian vegetables which cannot be found in Western countries, the recipes in this book have been confined to those that are easily obtainable in most parts of the world.

With the use of spices – and imagination – even potatoes can be transformed into quite an exotic vegetable, instead of being just an accompaniment to other food.

BAGHARA BAIGAN
(Aubergine Curry)

METRIC/IMPERIAL

4 medium aubergines
sweet oil for frying
1 tablespoon coriander seeds
4 dried red chillies
1 large onion, chopped
4 tablespoons freshly grated or 2 tablespoons desiccated coconut
1 clove garlic
1 teaspoon sesame seeds
50 g/2 oz tamarind
1 teaspoon turmeric
salt to taste
1 tablespoon brown sugar
1 tablespoon ghee or butter
2 green chillies
¼ teaspoon mustard seeds

Wash aubergines, then slit in quarters, lengthwise, keeping the stalk end whole. Fry in oil till they are a light brown. Remove and keep aside.

In a frying pan put 1 tablespoon oil and fry the coriander, dried chillies and chopped onion. Remove and grind them with the coconut and garlic to a paste. Roast the sesame seeds in a dry pan and grind to a powder. Soak the tamarind in 300 ml/½ pint warm water. Squeeze and strain through a sieve.

Mix the tamarind water with the paste and turmeric in a saucepan and bring to the boil. Add salt, aubergines and the sesame powder. Cover and cook for 5 minutes, then add the brown sugar. When the gravy is thick remove from heat.

In a frying pan heat the ghee and fry the green chillies and mustard seeds. When the seeds begin to splutter pour the contents of the frying pan over the curry. Stir and serve hot with rice.

AUBERGINE AND GREEN PEPPER CURRY

METRIC/IMPERIAL

1 large onion
450 g/1 lb aubergines
225 g/8 oz tomatoes
225 g/8 oz green peppers
75 g/3 oz butter or ghee
1 teaspoon turmeric
¼ teaspoon ginger powder
salt to taste
1 teaspoon garam masala

Slice onion finely. Wash aubergines, tomatoes and green peppers. Cut aubergines into 5-cm/2-inch pieces and tomatoes into quarters. Slice green peppers.

Heat the butter and fry the onion till pale golden. Add the aubergines, turmeric, ginger and salt and fry for 5 minutes. Then put in the tomatoes and green peppers and after stirring well cover and cook till the aubergines are tender. Sprinkle the garam masala over the curry and keep over a very low heat for another 2 minutes before serving.

AUBERGINE AND POTATO MOOLEE

METRIC/IMPERIAL

4 medium potatoes
4 aubergines
1 large coconut
2 medium onions
1 clove garlic
4 green chillies
2.5-cm/1-inch piece fresh ginger
50 g/2 oz ghee
½ teaspoon turmeric
salt to taste
2 tablespoons vinegar

Boil, peel and quarter the potatoes. Cook whole aubergines in boiling salted water till tender. Drain and cut into pieces the same size as the potatoes. Grate three-quarters of the coconut and steep in 300 ml/½ pint warm water. Grind the remaining coconut. Slice the onions. Chop the garlic. Slice the chillies and ginger into thin strips. Squeeze the steeped coconut and strain out the milk.

Heat the ghee and fry the onions until golden brown. Add the turmeric, ground coconut, ginger and garlic and cook for 3 minutes. Pour the coconut milk gradually into the mixture. Add the potatoes, aubergines, chillies and salt. Simmer for 5 minutes. Just before serving add the vinegar.

Serve with plain boiled rice.

FRIED AUBERGINES

METRIC/IMPERIAL

2 large aubergines
2 teaspoons turmeric
salt
ghee or vegetable fat for frying

Wash the aubergines and cut them across into thick rounds. Marinate them in a mixture of turmeric and salt for about 1 hour.

Press the slices between the hands to remove moisture. Heat the fat and fry. Drain before serving.

SPICED AUBERGINES

METRIC/IMPERIAL

450 g/1 lb large aubergines
2 tablespoons desiccated coconut
2 tablespoons hot milk
½ teaspoon sugar
4 tablespoons vinegar
2 onions
4 cloves garlic
2 green chillies
50 g/2 oz cooking fat
½ teaspoon turmeric
2 teaspoons salt
½ teaspoon ginger powder
150 ml/¼ pint yogurt

Wash and cut aubergines into rounds. Soak the coconut in the milk. Mix the sugar and vinegar. Slice the onions finely. Slice the garlic and chillies.

Heat the fat and fry the aubergine till brown. Add all the other ingredients and cook over a slow heat till aubergines are cooked.

GREEN BANANA CURRY

METRIC/IMPERIAL

25 g/1 oz tamarind
25 g/1 oz desiccated coconut
1 tablespoon hot milk
1 kg/2 lb green bananas
50 g/2 oz mustard seeds
25 g/1 oz sesame seeds
15 g/½ oz cooking fat
1 teaspoon turmeric
¼ teaspoon chilli powder
1 teaspoon salt

Soak the tamarind in 6 tablespoons water for 10 minutes, squeeze and strain the juice. Soak the coconut in the hot milk. Boil the bananas, peel and mash them. Grind the mustard seeds, the sesame seeds and coconut to a paste.

Heat the cooking fat and fry the paste, turmeric and chilli for 2 minutes. Add the tamarind juice and bring to the boil. Add the banana pulp and salt. Simmer for 5 minutes more.

GREEN BANANA AND POTATO STEW

METRIC/IMPERIAL

4 green bananas
4 medium potatoes
1 large onion
1 clove garlic
½ teaspoon ginger powder
½ teaspoon turmeric
¼ teaspoon chilli powder
25 g/1 oz cooking fat
3 bay leaves
½ teaspoon garam masala
½ teaspoon sugar
1 teaspoon salt
juice of ¼ lemon

Peel and cut the bananas into 3 pieces each. Boil till soft, drain and mash. Peel and dice potatoes, then boil and drain. Slice onion finely. Chop the garlic, add to the mashed bananas, ginger, turmeric and chilli and mix thoroughly.

Heat the fat and fry the bay leaves and garam masala for 1 minute, add the onions and fry till golden. Put in the banana mixture, potatoes, sugar and salt. Stir and fry for 5 minutes. Add lemon juice. Stir and serve.

FRENCH BEANS BHAJI

METRIC/IMPERIAL

675 g/1½ lb French beans
1 onion
50 g/2 oz ghee or butter
1 teaspoon turmeric
½ teaspoon chilli powder (optional)
salt to taste
½ teaspoon garam masala

Wash and break beans into small pieces. Chop onion.

Heat the ghee and fry the onion lightly; add the beans, turmeric, chilli if used and salt and fry for 3 minutes. Sprinkle over garam masala, cover and cook over a very low heat till the beans are soft.

THURARAN WITH FRENCH BEANS

METRIC/IMPERIAL

1 medium onion
3 green chillies
6 cashew nuts
450 g/1 lb French beans
2 teaspoons oil
½ teaspoon mustard seeds
1 teaspoon urad dal
2 curry leaves
¼ teaspoon turmeric
salt to taste
1 tablespoon desiccated or 2 tablespoons freshly grated coconut

Slice the onion. Chop the green chillies and cashew nuts. Slice the beans across into small pieces and blanch in a little water.

Heat the oil and fry the mustard seeds till they start spluttering. Add the urad dal and cashew nuts and fry. Then add the onions, curry leaves, chillies, turmeric and salt and fry till brown. Add the coconut then the beans. Mix thoroughly and serve.

FRENCH BEANS AND MUSHROOMS BHAJI

METRIC/IMPERIAL

225 g/8 oz French beans
100 g/4 oz mushrooms
1 medium onion
50 g/2 oz butter
½ teaspoon turmeric
½ teaspoon chilli powder (optional)
salt to taste

Break the beans into small pieces; slice the mushrooms. Slice the onion and fry in the butter till pale gold. Add the beans and the turmeric and fry for 2–3 minutes. Add the mushrooms, chilli if used and salt and cook covered over a very gentle heat till beans are soft.

CABBAGE CURRY

METRIC/IMPERIAL

1 large cabbage
1 tablespoon rice
3 potatoes
2 onions
½ green pepper or 2 green chillies
40 g/1½ oz butter or oil
½ teaspoon garam masala
¼ teaspoon ginger powder
¼ teaspoon turmeric
¼ teaspoon chilli powder
½ teaspoon sugar
1 teaspoon salt

Coarsely slice and steam the cabbage. Soak the rice in cold water for 30 minutes. Boil the potatoes and cut each into 8 pieces. Slice the onions and green pepper or chillies.

Heat the fat and fry the potatoes. Drain and keep aside. Fry the onions, garam masala and drained rice for 1 minute in the fat in the pan, then add the ginger, turmeric and chilli. Brown and add 300 ml/½ pint hot water and simmer till the rice is cooked.

Put in the cabbage, potatoes and sliced green pepper. Stir and add sugar and salt. Simmer till nearly all the liquid is gone. Serve hot.

BENGALI STYLE CABBAGE AND POTATOES

METRIC/IMPERIAL

450 g/1 lb potatoes
1 kg/2 lb cabbage
100 g/4 oz tomatoes
75 g/3 oz butter or margarine
1 teaspoon turmeric
¼ teaspoon ginger powder
1 teaspoon chilli powder
½ teaspoon sugar
salt to taste
½ teaspoon ground cloves
½ teaspoon ground cinnamon
½ teaspoon cardamom powder

Peel and cut potatoes into quarters. Shred the cabbage. Cut the tomatoes in quarters.

Heat the butter and fry the potatoes a pale brown. Drain and keep aside. Fry the cabbage in the butter and add the turmeric, ginger and chilli powder and stir well. Add the tomatoes, potatoes, sugar and salt and cook covered over gentle heat till tender. If required, add a little hot water. When cooked sprinkle with the ground cloves, cinnamon and cardamom powder and serve.

SOUTH INDIAN CABBAGE BHAJI

METRIC/IMPERIAL

1 kg/2 lb cabbage
50 g/2 oz ghee or oil
1 teaspoon mustard seeds
1 teaspoon urad dal
4 dried red chillies
pinch of brown sugar
salt to taste
1 tablespoon freshly grated coconut

Shred the cabbage. Heat the fat and add the mustard seeds, then the urad dal and chillies. Fry until the seeds splutter then add the cabbage, sugar and salt and stir well. Add 150 ml/¼ pint water and cover. Cook covered on medium heat for 10 minutes then remove lid for the water to evaporate. Serve with freshly grated coconut sprinkled on top.

THURARAN WITH CABBAGE

METRIC/IMPERIAL

1 medium onion
3 green chillies
6 cashew nuts
1 kg/2 lb cabbage
2 teaspoons oil
½ teaspoon mustard seeds
1 teaspoon urad dal
2 curry leaves
¼ teaspoon turmeric
1 tablespoon desiccated or 2 tablespoons freshly grated coconut
salt to taste

Slice the onion and chop the green chillies and the cashew nuts. Slice the cabbage finely and blanch in a little water. The cabbage should be crunchy so do not overcook.

Heat the oil and fry the mustard seeds till they start spluttering. Add the urad dal and cashew nuts and fry for 1 minute, then add the onion, curry leaves, chopped chillies and turmeric and fry till brown. Add the coconut and salt, then fold in the drained cabbage.

Mix lightly and serve.

GAJAR MATTAR
(Carrots and Peas)

METRIC/IMPERIAL

450 g/1 lb carrots
50 g/2 oz ghee or butter
½ teaspoon cummin seeds
½ teaspoon turmeric
1 teaspoon chilli powder
salt to taste
225 g/8 oz shelled peas

Scrape and cut carrots into rounds.

Heat ghee and fry the cummin seeds for 1 minute. Add the carrots, turmeric, chilli, salt and peas and fry for 2 minutes. Cover and cook over low heat till the vegetables are tender.

No water is necessary if this dish is cooked gently.

CAULIFLOWER COOKED IN YOGURT

METRIC/IMPERIAL

- 1 large cauliflower
- 3 onions
- 2 cloves garlic
- 2.5-cm/1-inch piece green ginger or ½ teaspoon ginger powder
- 300 ml/½ pint yogurt
- 1 teaspoon sugar
- 1 teaspoon salt
- 40 g/1½ oz ghee or cooking fat
- 1 teaspoon garam masala

Divide cauliflower into florets. Slice 1½ onions finely. Mince the remaining onions, garlic and fresh ginger. Put the yogurt in a bowl, add the minced ingredients, ginger powder if used, sugar and salt and beat with an egg beater. Marinate the cauliflower in the yogurt for 2 hours. Make sure the yogurt covers the florets all over.

Heat the fat and fry the onions until golden, add the cauliflower, all the yogurt and 150 ml/¼ pint hot water. Simmer till cauliflower is tender. Sprinkle with garam masala.

STUFFED KERALA
(Bitter Gourd)

METRIC/IMPERIAL

- 450 g/1 lb keralas
- salt to taste
- 225 g/8 oz onions
- 2 teaspoons pomegranate seeds
- 100 g/4 oz ghee
- 1 teaspoon chilli powder
- 1 teaspoon garam masala
- 3 tablespoons yogurt

Scrape the keralas, make a slit in the sides and remove the seeds. Rub the inside and outside with salt and leave for 1 hour. If the seeds are soft do not throw them away but use in the stuffing. Slice the onions finely. Grind the pomegranate seeds.

In 50 g/2 oz ghee fry the onions lightly and mix in the pomegranate powder, chilli, garam masala and more salt. Take off the heat and cool. Wash the keralas, dry and stuff them with the onion mixture. Tie them with thread.

Heat the rest of the ghee in a pan and add the keralas. Beat the yogurt till smooth, add salt and pour over the keralas. Cook over a slow heat, turning the vegetables till they are well browned.

LEEK BHAJI

METRIC/IMPERIAL

1 kg/2 lb leeks
salt to taste
50 g/2 oz butter
½ teaspoon cummin seeds
1 teaspoon turmeric
½ teaspoon ginger powder
½ teaspoon garam masala

Wash leeks and slice them into thin rounds. Soak in salted water for 15 minutes and wash again. Drain.

Heat the butter and add the cummin seeds. Fry for a few seconds then add the leeks, turmeric, ginger and more salt. Fry for 3–4 minutes; cover and cook over gentle heat till the leeks are tender. Sprinkle with garam masala and serve.

STUFFED VEGETABLE MARROW

Oven temperature: Moderately hot
190°C, 375°F, Gas Mark 5

METRIC/IMPERIAL

1 medium onion
40 g/1½ oz butter or margarine
225 g/8 oz minced meat
1 teaspoon coriander powder
1 teaspoon chilli powder
salt to taste
2 tablespoons yogurt
1 teaspoon garam masala
1 vegetable marrow
1 egg, beaten
225 g/8 oz tomatoes, skinned and chopped

Slice the onion and fry in the fat till pale gold. Add the minced meat and fry for 5 minutes. Add the coriander, chilli, salt and yogurt and fry over gentle heat till the meat is a rich brown. Keep adding a little water while cooking. When the meat is cooked sprinkle the garam masala over it.

Wash the marrow. If the outer skin is soft, do not peel the marrow, but do if it is tough. Cut a piece from the top and scoop out all the seeds.

Add the well-beaten egg to the mince and stuff the marrow with the mixture. Replace the piece from the top and secure with wooden cocktail sticks or skewers. Grease the marrow, wrap it in foil and bake in the oven for 1 hour. Make a sauce with the liquid from the marrow and the tomatoes and serve with the marrow.

MARROW BHAJI

METRIC/IMPERIAL

1 young marrow
1 teaspoon cummin seeds
2 green chillies or
1 teaspoon chilli powder
50 g/2 oz butter
salt to taste
½ teaspoon sugar
1 teaspoon rice flour

Wash the marrow and cut into 3.5-cm/1½-inch pieces. In a dry frying pan roast the cummin seeds and grind to a powder. Chop the chillies.

Heat the butter and add the chillies, marrow, salt and sugar and cook for 10 minutes in an uncovered pan. Cover and cook gently till tender, then add the rice flour mixed in a little water to form a paste.

Cook for 5–6 minutes then add the powdered cummin and serve.

MUSHROOM BHAJI

METRIC/IMPERIAL

350 g/12 oz mushrooms
2 large onions
100 g/4 oz ghee or butter
1 teaspoon turmeric
1 teaspoon chilli powder
1 clove garlic, chopped (optional)
salt to taste

Wash and dry the mushrooms. If large cut into pieces. Slice onions finely.

Heat the ghee and fry the onions till they are soft and half cooked. Add the turmeric, chilli and the garlic if used and fry for 1 minute. Add the mushrooms and salt and cook over gentle heat till mushrooms are tender.

MUSHROOM STALKS BHAJI

METRIC/IMPERIAL

450 g/1 lb mushroom stalks
2 onions
75 g/3 oz ghee
1 teaspoon turmeric
1 teaspoon chilli powder
salt to taste
½ teaspoon garam masala

Wash and clean mushroom stalks. Slice onions finely.

Heat the ghee and fry the onions till they appear glazed. Add the turmeric, chilli and the stalks and fry for 1 minute. Add salt and garam masala, cover and simmer over low heat till the stalks are tender.

No water is required if this dish is cooked gently over low heat.

CURRIED MUSHROOM STALKS

METRIC/IMPERIAL

450 g/1 lb mushroom stalks
2 medium onions
1 clove garlic
225 g/8 oz tomatoes
75 g/3 oz ghee
1 teaspoon turmeric
1 teaspoon coriander powder
1 teaspoon chilli powder
1 teaspoon paprika
¼ teaspoon ginger powder
salt to taste
1 teaspoon garam masala

Wash the mushroom stalks thoroughly. Slice the onions finely. Chop the garlic and quarter the tomatoes.

Heat the ghee and fry the onions till they are pale gold. Add the garlic, turmeric, coriander, chilli, paprika and ginger and fry for 2 minutes. Add the tomatoes and fry for 5 minutes. Add mushroom stalks and salt and cook covered over a gentle heat till the stalks are tender. Sprinkle with garam masala, cover for 2 minutes and serve.

OKRA BHAJI

METRIC/IMPERIAL

450 g/1 lb okra
75 g/3 oz ghee or butter
1 medium onion, sliced
1 teaspoon turmeric
salt and black pepper to taste

Wash and dry okra, then cut into small pieces.

Heat the ghee and fry the sliced onion till it is very pale golden. Add the okra and the turmeric, fry 1 minute then add the salt and pepper.

Cook over a very low heat till tender.

OKRA CURRY

METRIC/IMPERIAL

40 g/1½ oz cooking fat
4 onions, sliced
1 teaspoon ginger powder
½ teaspoon coriander powder
1 teaspoon turmeric
½ teaspoon dry mustard
¼ teaspoon chilli powder
½ teaspoon curry powder
1 teaspoon garlic salt
8 bay leaves
1 (200-g/7-oz) can okra, well drained
450 ml/¾ pint tamarind water (see page 18)
50 g/2 oz desiccated coconut soaked in 2 tablespoons hot milk
1 teaspoon salt

Heat the cooking fat in a saucepan and fry the onions till a light cream colour. Add the ginger, coriander, turmeric, mustard, chilli, curry powder and garlic salt and fry for 5 minutes. Now fry the bay leaves for another 2 minutes, stirring constantly to prevent burning. Put in the okra, tamarind water, coconut and salt.

Bring to the boil, then lower heat and simmer gently for 10 minutes.

OKRA STEW

METRIC/IMPERIAL

1 onion
½ green pepper
25 g/1 oz cooking fat
1 (200-g/7-oz) can okra, well drained
1 teaspoon salt
1 teaspoon turmeric
2 teaspoons gram flour
½ teaspoon coriander powder
½ teaspoon ginger powder
150 ml/¼ pint buttermilk

Slice the onion. Chop green pepper finely.

Heat the fat and fry the onion until almond in colour. Add okra and fry gently for 5 minutes. Put in all other ingredients except buttermilk. Fry gently for 5 minutes. Add buttermilk and bring to the boil. Simmer for 15 minutes till half the liquid is absorbed.

PIAZ BHAJI
(Onion Bhaji)

METRIC/IMPERIAL

450 g/1 lb onions
50 g/2 oz ghee or butter
½ teaspoon turmeric
1 teaspoon chilli powder
1 teaspoon garam masala
salt to taste
few coriander leaves (optional)

Slice the onions thickly. Heat the ghee and add the onions, turmeric, chilli, garam masala and salt and fry for 3–4 minutes over brisk heat.

Lower heat and cook covered till onions are soft. Sprinkle with coriander leaves if liked and serve.

PEAS AND OKRA IN YOGURT

METRIC/IMPERIAL

1 (113-g/4-oz) packet frozen peas
50 g/2 oz desiccated coconut
2 tablespoons hot milk
50 g/2 oz cooking fat
1 (200-g/7-oz) can okra, well drained
1 teaspoon turmeric
¼ teaspoon chilli powder
½ teaspoon ginger powder
½ teaspoon coriander powder
150 ml/¼ pint yogurt
salt to taste

Boil the peas. Drain. Soak coconut in milk.

Heat the fat and fry the okra and peas for 5 minutes. Add spices. Fry 5 minutes on a low heat. Mix yogurt with salt and coconut, then add to saucepan with the other ingredients. Simmer till half the liquid is absorbed.

MATTAR PANIR

METRIC/IMPERIAL

225 g/8 oz panir (see page 18)
1 large onion
225 g/8 oz tomatoes
100 g/4 oz butter, ghee or margarine
1 teaspoon turmeric
1 teaspoon ginger powder
2 teaspoons coriander powder
1 teaspoon chilli powder
450 g/1 lb shelled peas
300 ml/½ pint whey
salt to taste

Cut the cheese into 2.5-cm/1-inch pieces. Slice the onion finely and chop the tomatoes.

Heat the fat and fry the pieces of cheese till pale golden; remove and keep aside. In the same fat, fry the onion till pale golden. Add the spices and fry for a minute or so, then add the tomatoes, peas, whey and salt.

Cook over low heat till the peas are tender, and add the cheese. Simmer for 15 minutes.

PARSNIP BHAJI

METRIC/IMPERIAL

- 450 g/1 lb parsnips
- 1 small onion
- ½ green pepper
- 50 g/2 oz ghee or butter
- ½ teaspoon turmeric
- ½ teaspoon cummin powder
- 1 teaspoon chilli powder
- salt to taste

Peel and dice the parsnips. Slice the onion. Shred the green pepper.

Heat the ghee and fry the onion until golden brown. Add the turmeric, cummin, chilli and the parsnips. Add 3 tablespoons water and salt to taste and simmer till the parsnips are cooked.

Garnish with the shredded green pepper.

PEA AND CASHEW NUT STEW

METRIC/IMPERIAL

- 8 small onions
- 2 cloves garlic
- 2.5-cm/1-inch piece ginger
- ¼ green pepper
- 450 g/1 lb shelled peas
- 225 g/8 oz cashew nuts
- 25 g/1 oz cooking fat
- 2 teaspoons garam masala
- 1 teaspoon rice flour
- 150 ml/¼ pint thick coconut milk (see page 17)
- salt to taste

Peel onions. Chop garlic coarsely and crush. Grate ginger. Chop green pepper. Boil peas. Fry cashew nuts in 15 g/½ oz of the fat.

Heat remaining cooking fat in saucepan and fry the garam masala, rice flour, ginger and garlic. Add the onions and fry till cream coloured. Pour in coconut milk. Add salt, peas, nuts and green pepper. Cook gently till peas are done.

CURRIED GREEN PEPPERS

METRIC/IMPERIAL

- 2 onions, sliced
- 25 g/1 oz cooking fat
- 4 bay leaves
- 1 teaspoon mustard seeds
- 1 small piece ginger, sliced
- 2 cloves garlic, sliced
- 8 green peppers, sliced
- 2½ tablespoons thick tamarind water (see page 18)
- 1 teaspoon salt
- ½ teaspoon sugar

Fry 1 sliced onion until brown and crisp in the cooking fat, drain and set aside.

Then fry the other sliced onion, bay leaves, mustard seeds, ginger and garlic. Then add the green peppers, tamarind water, salt and sugar. Bring to the boil and simmer gently till peppers are soft.

Sprinkle the crisply fried onion over and serve with white rice and yogurt.

ALU DUM

METRIC/IMPERIAL

- 1 tablespoon coriander seeds
- ¼ teaspoon peppercorns
- ½ teaspoon turmeric
- ½ teaspoon ginger powder
- 1 teaspoon chilli powder
- 2 tablespoons yogurt
- 450 g/1 lb potatoes
- 100 g/4 oz ghee or butter
- ½ teaspoon cummin seeds
- 1 teaspoon sugar
- salt to taste
- ¼ teaspoon ground cloves
- ½ teaspoon ground cinnamon
- ½ teaspoon cardamom powder

Roast coriander seeds and peppercorns in a dry frying pan and grind. Mix this powder to a paste with turmeric, ginger, chilli powder and a little water. Add the yogurt to the paste.

Boil the unpeeled potatoes till half done. Peel and coat them with the paste.

Heat the fat and fry the cummin seeds for 1 minute. Add the potatoes, sugar, salt and a little water and cook covered till the potatoes are tender and dry. Sprinkle with the ground cloves, cinnamon and cardamom and keep covered till ready to serve.

ALU TARI
(Potato Curry)

METRIC/IMPERIAL

450 g/1 lb potatoes
225 g/8 oz tomatoes
50 g/2 oz ghee or butter
1 teaspoon turmeric
1 teaspoon cummin seeds
salt to taste
1 teaspoon chilli powder

Peel and dice the potatoes. Chop the tomatoes.

Melt the fat and add the potatoes, turmeric, cummin and salt and fry for 5 minutes. Add the tomatoes and chilli powder and fry for 2–3 minutes.

Add enough hot water to cover the potatoes. Bring to the boil and simmer till tender. There should be plenty of gravy.

ALU PUNJABI

METRIC/IMPERIAL

450 g/1 lb potatoes
50 g/2 oz butter or ghee
½ teaspoon mustard seeds
½ teaspoon fenugreek seeds
½ teaspoon cummin seeds
2 dried red chillies
½ teaspoon turmeric
salt and pepper to taste

Peel and dice the potatoes.

Heat the fat and fry the mustard seeds, fenugreek seeds, cummin seeds and dried chillies. Add the potatoes, mix well and cover. After 2 minutes add the turmeric, salt and pepper. Mix thoroughly, then add 3 tablespoons water and cook till it is a thick paste.

This is served with puris.

ALU MATTAR SUKHE
(Dry Potatoes and Peas)

METRIC/IMPERIAL

1 large onion
75 g/3 oz butter or ghee
450 g/1 lb potatoes
1 teaspoon turmeric
1 teaspoon chilli powder
½ teaspoon ginger powder
½ teaspoon cummin powder
225 g/8 oz shelled peas
salt to taste
1 teaspoon garam masala

Slice onions finely and fry them a golden brown in the butter or ghee. Add the peeled and diced potatoes and all the spices except the garam masala. Fry for 5 minutes then add the peas and salt and cook very slowly covered till the vegetables are cooked.

No water is needed if this is cooked over a very low heat with the pan covered. When nearly ready sprinkle with the garam masala.

ALU BARI

METRIC/IMPERIAL

50 g/2 oz ghee
1 large bari*
1 medium onion
450 g/1 lb potatoes
½ teaspoon turmeric
½ teaspoon ginger powder
salt to taste
2 large tomatoes (optional)

**Baris are made from urad dal, ground into a paste and mixed with a special kind of marrow and spices, then shaped into balls and dried.*

Heat the ghee and fry the bari whole till brown, then remove from pan.

Slice the onion finely and fry in the same ghee till glazed. Peel and halve the potatoes and fry for 5 minutes. Add the turmeric, ginger and salt and fry for 1 minute. Cut the tomatoes into quarters and add to the pan. Cook for 5 minutes then add the bari and 600 ml/1 pint warm water. Bring to the boil then simmer for 10 minutes or until the bari and potatoes are cooked. This is a typical Punjabi dish and the bari should be the kind made in the Punjab.

ALU METHI

METRIC/IMPERIAL

450 g/1 lb potatoes
2 teaspoons dried or 2 handfuls fresh fenugreek
50 g/2 oz ghee or butter
½ teaspoon turmeric
1 teaspoon chilli powder
salt to taste

Peel and cut the potatoes into cubes. If dried fenugreek is used, soak in a little water and strain. If fresh leaves are used, wash and chop them.

Heat the ghee, add potatoes and turmeric and fry for 3 minutes. Add prepared fenugreek, chilli and salt and fry for another 3 minutes. Lower heat and cook covered till potatoes are cooked.

ALU DAHI

METRIC/IMPERIAL

450 g/1 lb potatoes
25 g/1 oz ghee or butter
¼ teaspoon turmeric
1 teaspoon chilli powder or 2 green chillies, chopped
4 tablespoons yogurt
1 clove garlic
salt to taste

Boil potatoes. Peel and dice them.

Heat the fat, add turmeric, chilli and yogurt. Chop the garlic, add to the spices and fry for 1 minute. Then add the potatoes and salt. Cover and cook gently for 5 minutes.

KHATTA ALU
(Sour Potatoes)

METRIC/IMPERIAL

walnut-size piece tamarind
450 g/1 lb potatoes
50 g/2 oz ghee
¼ teaspoon turmeric
1 teaspoon chilli powder
salt to taste
2 teaspoons garam masala

Soak the tamarind in 3 tablespoons water for 15–20 minutes then squeeze to extract the juice and strain. Boil, peel and dice the potatoes.

Heat the ghee and fry the turmeric and chilli for 1 minute. Add the potatoes and salt and when the potatoes are well mixed add the garam masala and the tamarind water. Cook till dry.

SUKHE ALU CHILKE WALE
(Dry Potatoes in Jackets)

METRIC/IMPERIAL

1 kg/2 lb very small new potatoes
75 g/3 oz ghee or oil
1 large onion, finely chopped
1 teaspoon chilli powder
1 teaspoon turmeric
salt to taste
2 teaspoons garam masala

Wash potatoes thoroughly. Heat the ghee and fry the onion till light brown then add the potatoes, chilli, turmeric and salt and cook for 5 minutes. Cover and cook over low heat till nearly done.

Add the garam masala and cook till the potatoes are tender. This is a very delicious dish.

ALU GOBI
(Potato and Cauliflower)

METRIC/IMPERIAL

225 g/8 oz potatoes
1 cauliflower
100 g/4 oz butter or ghee
½ teaspoon cummin seeds
2.5-cm/1-inch piece green ginger, sliced thinly, or ¼ teaspoon ginger powder
1 teaspoon turmeric
1 teaspoon chilli powder
salt to taste
½ teaspoon black pepper

Peel and dice potatoes. Divide cauliflower into florets of the same size. Wash vegetables and drain.

Heat fat, add the potatoes, cummin seeds, ginger, turmeric, chilli and salt and fry for 2 minutes. Add the cauliflower and fry all together for 5 minutes. Cover and cook on a very low heat till cooked. Sprinkle with freshly ground black pepper and serve. No water should be necessary.

FRIED POTATO CAKES

METRIC/IMPERIAL

450 g/1 lb potatoes
40 g/1½ oz gram flour
40 g/1½ oz rice flour
25 g/1 oz desiccated coconut
½ green pepper
½ teaspoon coriander powder
1 teaspoon turmeric
½ teaspoon ginger powder
½ teaspoon cummin powder
1 teaspoon salt
225 g/8 oz cooking fat

Peel, boil and mash potatoes. Make a batter of the gram and rice flour with a little cold water. Soak coconut in 2 teaspoons hot water. Chop green pepper very finely. All the ingredients should be mixed with the mashed potatoes except the batter and fat. Mix well with a wooden spoon, taking care the spices and salt are evenly mixed into the potatoes. Make into balls the size of small walnuts, then flatten into cakes.

Dip them in the batter and fry in hot fat. Deep frying makes them lighter and tastier.

SAMOSAS

METRIC/IMPERIAL

vegetable fat for deep frying

for pastry:

450 g/1 lb plain flour
½ teaspoon baking powder
1 teaspoon salt
25 g/1 oz melted butter or ghee
4 tablespoons yogurt

filling:

50 g/2 oz ghee or butter
1 small onion, chopped
450 g/1 lb potatoes, boiled
2 green chillies
salt to taste
1 teaspoon garam masala

To make the pastry, sift the flour, baking powder and salt into a bowl. Add the melted butter or ghee and the yogurt and make into a pliable dough. Knead thoroughly so that the dough is smooth.

To make filling, heat the 50 g/2 oz ghee and fry the chopped onion for 2 minutes. Add the potatoes and chillies cut into small pieces and fry for 5 minutes. Add salt and garam masala and mix thoroughly. Cool.

Knead dough again. Take small walnut size pieces of the dough and make into round balls. Flatten and roll out on a floured board. Make thin rounds the size of a saucer. Cut each in half. Make into a cone, seal edges with water and fill with potato mixture. Wet open edges with water and press together.

When all the samosas are filled, fry in hot deep fat till they are crisp and golden. These make delicious snacks.

SPICED MASHED POTATOES

METRIC/IMPERIAL

225 g/8 oz potatoes
¼ green pepper
15 g/½ oz cooking fat
7 g/¼ oz masoor dal
1 teaspoon mustard seeds
small piece ginger
2 teaspoons salt
½ teaspoon turmeric
juice of ½ lemon
15 g/½ oz desiccated coconut

Peel, boil and mash potatoes. Slice green pepper finely.

Heat fat in a frying pan and fry the dal and mustard seeds till the mustard seeds start to splutter and burst. Then put in the green pepper, ginger, salt and turmeric. Fry for 5 minutes, stirring to prevent burning. Put in potatoes. Stir well to mix. Remove from the heat.

Add lemon juice. Sprinkle with desiccated coconut and beat well with an egg beater.

PUMPKIN AND POTATOES

METRIC/IMPERIAL

2 tablespoons chana dal
100 g/4 oz potatoes
225 g/8 oz pumpkin flesh
50 g/2 oz ghee or butter
½ teaspoon mustard seeds
½ teaspoon onion seeds
½ teaspoon cummin seeds
½ teaspoon ginger powder
2 green chillies, chopped
½ teaspoon sugar
salt to taste

Soak dal overnight. Peel and dice potatoes. Dice the pumpkin.

Heat the ghee or butter, fry the pumpkin and set aside.

Fry the mustard seeds, onion seeds, cummin seeds and ginger in the fat remaining for 3 minutes and add the chana dal, potatoes, chopped green chillies, sugar and salt. Add 150 ml/¼ pint water and simmer till cooked. Add the pumpkin, mix thoroughly and serve.

SPICED SPINACH PURÉE

Oven temperature: Hot
220°C, 425°F, Gas Mark 7

METRIC/IMPERIAL

2 large bunches spinach
2 onions
¼ green pepper
25 g/1 oz cooking fat
salt and pepper to taste
eggs

Clean and wash spinach. Remove stems and chop. Chop onions and green pepper.

Heat the fat in a saucepan. Add the onions and green pepper. Fry until almond in colour. Put in the spinach and simmer until dry. Add salt and pepper. Stir and mash and remove from heat.

If desired spread spinach in a frying pan. Add 3 tablespoons hot water. Break as many eggs as required on it, one at a time, and simmer gently till eggs are set. Alternatively the spinach can be put into an ovenproof dish, and, after the eggs are broken on it, put into the oven till eggs are set, about 20 minutes.

GUJRATI POTATOES

METRIC/IMPERIAL

450 g/1 lb potatoes
15 g/½ oz tamarind
1 tablespoon brown sugar
50 g/2 oz ghee or butter
1 teaspoon mustard seeds
½ teaspoon turmeric
½ teaspoon chilli powder
2 teaspoons coriander powder
salt to taste
2 green chillies, sliced
2 tablespoons desiccated coconut

Peel and dice the potatoes. Put the tamarind in 3 tablespoons water, squeeze and strain. Add the sugar to the juice and mix.

Heat the fat and fry the mustard seeds till they splutter and burst. Add the potatoes, spices and salt and fry for 1–2 minutes. Cover and cook over gentle heat till potatoes are cooked. Add the tamarind juice, the sliced green chillies and the coconut and cook for another 5 minutes.

PARSEE SPINACH

METRIC/IMPERIAL

4 large onions
2 cloves garlic
1 teaspoon ginger powder
¼ green pepper or 1 green chilli
50 g/2 oz olive oil
½ teaspoon cummin powder
1 kg/2 lb spinach
¼ teaspoon chilli powder
¼ teaspoon garam masala
¼ teaspoon turmeric
½ teaspoon salt

Slice the onions finely. Pound garlic with ginger to a paste. Chop the green pepper or chilli. Heat oil and fry onions until golden brown. Add garlic and fry for 3 minutes, then add the green pepper and cummin and fry, stirring, for 2 minutes. Add the washed spinach and rest of the ingredients.

Cook over low heat till spinach is cooked. Do not cover, but keep stirring till ready. Add 1 tablespoon hot water if necessary.

SPINACH WITH POTATOES

METRIC/IMPERIAL

1 kg/2 lb spinach
225 g/8 oz potatoes (new if available)
50 g/2 oz butter
1 large onion, sliced
1 teaspoon cummin seeds
2 green or 2 dried red chillies
½ teaspoon ginger powder
salt to taste

Wash the spinach. Peel or scrape the potatoes and cut into quarters.

Heat the butter and fry the onion until golden. Add the potatoes, cummin seeds, chopped green chillies or whole red chillies and the ginger, and cook for 5 minutes, stirring all the time. Add the spinach and cover the pan for 2 minutes. Add the salt and cook uncovered till the water is absorbed. Cover and cook over very gentle heat till ready.

SPINACH BHAJI

METRIC/IMPERIAL

1 kg/2 lb spinach
50 g/2 oz butter
1 onion, sliced
4 dried red chillies
1 teaspoon cummin seeds
½ teaspoon ginger powder
salt to taste

Pick over the spinach, remove thick stalks and wash.

Heat the butter and fry the onion till light brown. Add the chillies and cummin seeds and fry for 2–3 minutes. Add the spinach and ginger and cook covered for 5 minutes. Add salt and cook uncovered till liquid is nearly all absorbed. Cover and finish cooking over very gentle heat till done.

BHAJI OF SPRING GREENS

METRIC/IMPERIAL

1 kg/2 lb spring greens
salt to taste
pinch of bicarbonate of soda
50 g/2 oz butter
1 onion, sliced
1 teaspoon cummin seeds
1 teaspoon mustard seeds
4 dried red chillies
½ teaspoon turmeric
½ teaspoon ginger powder

Wash and chop the greens. Boil in salted water with a pinch of bicarbonate of soda till tender. Drain.

Heat the fat and fry the onion till soft with the cummin, mustard and chillies. Add the greens, turmeric and ginger and cook for 5 minutes in a covered pan. Add salt and cook uncovered over a brisk heat till the liquid is gone.

VEGETABLE CURRY (1)

METRIC/IMPERIAL

2 potatoes
3 large carrots
100 g/4 oz green peas
100 g/4 oz green beans
5-cm/2-inch piece green ginger
¼ green pepper
2 large onions
3 cloves garlic
100 g/4 oz butter
1 teaspoon turmeric
salt and black pepper to taste
1 tablespoon flour
300 ml/½ pint thick coconut milk (see page 17)
300 ml/½ pint milk
juice of 2 lemons
1 tablespoon vinegar

Boil and dice potatoes and carrots. Boil peas and beans. Cut beans in small pieces, ginger and green pepper in thin strips. Chop onions and garlic in very fine slices.

Melt butter and fry the onions and garlic a pale golden colour. Add the green pepper and ginger and fry 10 minutes, stirring often. Add the turmeric, salt, pepper and flour. Stir. Add the coconut milk and plain milk. Simmer slowly until gravy is reduced by almost half. Add the lemon juice and vinegar and then the boiled vegetables. Remove from heat after 10 minutes.

Note: Fillets of boiled fish or hard-boiled eggs cut in half can be added to this curry at the same time as the vegetables.

VEGETABLE CURRY (2)

METRIC/IMPERIAL

1 large onion
1 clove garlic
225 g/8 oz tiny or medium potatoes
225 g/8 oz tomatoes
50 g/2 oz ghee or butter
¼ teaspoon ginger powder
1 teaspoon turmeric
1 teaspoon coriander powder
1 teaspoon paprika
½ teaspoon garam masala
3 green chillies, chopped, or 1 teaspoon chilli powder
salt to taste
1 (340-g/12-oz) packet frozen mixed peas, carrots and French beans

Chop the onion and garlic. Peel the potatoes. If medium potatoes are used, cut them into small pieces. Quarter the tomatoes.

Heat the ghee and lightly fry the onion and garlic. Add the spices, chillies, salt and half the tomatoes and cook over gentle heat till the water is gone. Add the potatoes and fry for 2 minutes. Add the frozen vegetables, the remaining tomatoes and 150 ml/¼ pint water.

Simmer till the vegetables are tender.

SIMPLE BHAJI OF FROZEN MIXED VEGETABLES AND POTATOES

METRIC/IMPERIAL

450 g/1 lb potatoes
1 onion
50 g/2 oz ghee or butter
salt to taste
pinch turmeric
1 teaspoon chilli powder
1 (340-g/12-oz) packet frozen mixed vegetables

Peel the potatoes and dice. Slice the onion. Heat the ghee and add the potatoes and onion. Add salt, turmeric and chilli powder and cook till nearly tender. Thaw the frozen vegetables. Wash and drain them and add to the potatoes. Cook for another 10 minutes and serve hot.

Curry Accompaniments

Raitas, which have a yogurt base, are the most usual accompaniment to curries and are eaten in larger quantities than chutneys or pickles. Together with salads, they are easy and quick to make.

Popadams are very popular and can be bought either plain or spiced with black pepper and cummin seeds.

RASAM
(Pepper Water)

METRIC/IMPERIAL

1 teaspoon cummin seeds
1 teaspoon mustard seeds
10 dried red chillies
1 teaspoon peppercorns
4 cloves garlic
50 g/2 oz tamarind
½ teaspoon turmeric
1 small onion, sliced
2 teaspoons oil or ghee

Fry the cummin and mustard seeds and chillies in a dry pan and grind coarsely. Grind the peppercorns coarsely. Chop the garlic.

Pour 900 ml/1½ pints water into a saucepan and add the tamarind, garlic, turmeric, peppercorns and the ground seeds. Bring to the boil, remove immediately from the heat and strain.

Fry sliced onion in the oil or ghee and pour over the pepper water. Serve with boiled rice and curry.

PAPAR-PAPAD OR POPADAMS

Popadams can be bought at stores selling Indian preparations. They are paper-thin dry cakes made from potatoes or lentils, and are delicious. Some are mild, others hot, seasoned with pepper and spices. They are an accompaniment to Indian food but are also used as a savoury. Cooking papar is a tricky business as it curls up and doubles its size when fried in hot fat or when roasted over a charcoal fire. The secret is to keep turning it so that it remains flat. It is cooked very quickly, in a few seconds.

POTATO RAITA

METRIC/IMPERIAL

225 g/8 oz potatoes
450 ml/¾ pint yogurt
2 green chillies
salt to taste
½ teaspoon chilli powder
½ teaspoon garam masala

Boil and dice the potatoes. Beat the yogurt till smooth and, if very thick, thin with a little milk. Chop the green chillies. Add the potatoes and chillies to the yogurt and mix well. Add salt to taste. Put in a dish and sprinkle with chilli powder and garam masala.

CUCUMBER RAITA

METRIC/IMPERIAL

1 small cucumber
salt to taste
450 ml/¾ pint yogurt
2 green chillies (optional)
½ teaspoon chilli powder
½ teaspoon garam masala

If the cucumber is tender, grate it without peeling; otherwise, peel and then grate. Sprinkle with salt and leave for an hour or so. Beat the yogurt till smooth and if too thick add a little milk. Chop the green chillies. Squeeze out the water from the cucumber and add the cucumber to the yogurt. Add the chopped chillies and taste. If more salt is required add that also. Put the mixture in a dish. Sprinkle with chilli powder and garam masala and serve.

AUBERGINE RAITA

Oven temperature: Moderate
180°C, 350°F, Gas Mark 4

METRIC/IMPERIAL

450 g/1 lb aubergines
olive oil
1 small onion, chopped
½ teaspoon chilli powder
1 teaspoon garam masala
2 green chillies
450 ml/¾ pint yogurt
salt to taste

Rub oil over the whole washed aubergines and bake in the oven or cook under a grill till the aubergines are soft. Cool and take off the outer skin.

Mash the flesh and add chopped onion, chilli powder and garam masala. Chop the green chillies. Beat the yogurt till smooth and add to the aubergine mixture with the chillies and salt.

TAMARIND AND POTATO RAITA

METRIC/IMPERIAL

450 g/1 lb potatoes
100 g/4 oz tamarind
sugar and salt to taste
1 teaspoon chilli powder
1 teaspoon garam masala
2 green chillies, chopped (optional)

Boil potatoes, cool, peel and dice. Soak the tamarind in 300 ml/½ pint warm water for 30 minutes. Squeeze out all the pulp and strain the tamarind. Add sugar, salt and chilli powder to the juice. Mix in the potatoes. Taste to see if any more sugar or salt is required. Put in a dish, sprinkle with garam masala and chopped green chillies.

MARROW RAITA (1)

METRIC/IMPERIAL

450 g/1 lb marrow
1 small onion
2 green chillies
450 ml/¾ pint yogurt
salt to taste
1 teaspoon garam masala

Peel marrow and grate it. Chop the onion and the green chillies. Cook marrow in boiling water for 2 minutes. Drain. Beat the yogurt and add the marrow, onion, chillies and salt. Pour into a dish and sprinkle with garam masala.

MARROW RAITA (2)

METRIC/IMPERIAL

675-g–1-kg/1½–2-lb young marrow
salt to taste
450 ml/¾ pint yogurt
½ teaspoon chilli powder
½ teaspoon garam masala

Peel and grate the marrow. Put in boiling salted water and remove as soon as the marrow is tender, about 2 minutes. Do not overcook. Drain the marrow. Beat the yogurt till smooth. Mix the marrow and yogurt. Add salt to taste. Put into serving dish and sprinkle with chilli and garam masala.

KARHI
(Yogurt Curry)

METRIC/IMPERIAL

450 ml/¾ pint yogurt
50 g/2 oz gram flour
1 teaspoon turmeric
½ teaspoon ginger powder
1 teaspoon garam masala
2 teaspoons chilli powder
salt to taste
1 medium onion
25 g/1 oz ghee or butter

for pakoras:
225 g/8 oz gram flour
½ teaspoon turmeric
pinch of bicarbonate of soda
salt to taste
vegetable fat for frying

Put the yogurt in a large bowl and beat till smooth. Add 600 ml/1 pint cold water. Sift the gram flour and add gradually to the liquid with the turmeric, ginger, garam masala, chilli and salt. Mix well so that no lumps remain then strain into a pan. Bring to the boil, stirring all the time. Simmer gently for 20 minutes. Remove from the heat.

To make pakoras, sift the gram flour, turmeric, bicarbonate of soda and salt into a bowl. Add sufficient water to make a paste of dropping consistency. Beat hard. Heat plenty of fat and drop teaspoonfuls of batter into it. Fry till brown and crisp. Drain and keep aside.

Slice the onion finely. Put the pakoras into the hot karhi 10 minutes before serving and simmer. The karhi should be as thick as lentil soup.

In a frying pan heat the ghee and fry the onion until golden. Pour over the karhi and serve.

POTATO AND YOGURT PUREE
Oven temperature: Moderately hot
200°C, 400°F, Gas Mark 6

METRIC/IMPERIAL

¼ green pepper
4 mint leaves
12 coriander leaves
1 kg/2 lb potatoes
¼ teaspoon cummin powder
½ teaspoon garam masala
1 teaspoon salt
juice of 1 lemon
15 g/½ oz cooking fat
150 ml/¼ pint yogurt

Chop green pepper, mint and coriander leaves finely. Bake potatoes in the oven then mash. Mix all the ingredients except fat and yogurt with potatoes.

Heat fat and fry mixture gently, stirring all the time. Remove from heat and mix in the yogurt with an egg beater.

GREEN CHUTNEY WITH YOGURT

METRIC/IMPERIAL

½ green pepper
2 tablespoons coriander or watercress leaves
3 cloves garlic
300 ml/½ pint yogurt
1½ teaspoons cummin powder
½ teaspoon sugar

Chop finely the green pepper and coriander or watercress leaves. Chop the garlic. Mix the yogurt in a bowl and beat till thin. Mix all the ingredients together in the bowl and serve with pulaos or white rice.

BAIGAN BHURTHA
(Aubergine)

METRIC/IMPERIAL

450 g/1 lb aubergines
olive oil
1 medium onion
2 green chillies
25 g/1 oz butter or ghee
½ teaspoon cummin seeds
salt to taste

Rub the washed aubergines with oil and grill until the skin is scorched and brown. Cool and remove the skin. Mash the pulp. Chop the onion and the chillies.

Heat the ghee and fry the onions for a few minutes till lightly browned. Add the cummin seeds, aubergine pulp and chopped chillies. Fry for 3 minutes. Add salt, stir and remove from heat.

MARROW BHURTHA

METRIC/IMPERIAL

1 kg/2 lb marrow
2 green chillies
225 g/8 oz onions
1 teaspoon chilli powder
salt to taste
50 g/2 oz ghee
1 teaspoon cummin seeds
1 clove garlic

Peel, then boil the marrow in 150 ml/¼ pint water. When soft remove from heat, drain and mash. Slice the green chillies. Chop the onions. Add the onions, chilli powder and salt to the marrow.

In a clean pan heat the ghee and fry the cummin seeds and garlic. Press the clove of garlic to the sides of the pan to extract the flavour, then remove it from the pan. Add the marrow to the ghee and cook for 5 minutes. Serve with a garnish of the sliced chillies.

TOMATO BHURTHA

METRIC/IMPERIAL

4 ripe tomatoes	2–3 green chillies
1 large onion	salt and sugar to taste

Scald the tomatoes in boiling water. Remove skins and mash with a fork, removing the hard parts. Chop the onion and the chillies very finely and mix with the tomatoes. Add sugar and salt to taste.

POTATO BHURTHA

METRIC/IMPERIAL

4 medium potatoes	lemon juice and salt to taste
1 large onion	1 teaspoon mustard oil
2 green chillies	

Peel the potatoes and dice. Boil in salted water and mash to a smooth paste. Chop the onion and chillies and mix with the potato. Add lemon juice, salt and oil. If no mustard oil is available, a little melted butter can be used instead.

CABBAGE SALAD

METRIC/IMPERIAL

450 g/1 lb cabbage	½ teaspoon chilli powder
1 small onion	juice of 1 lemon
3 tablespoons desiccated coconut	salt and sugar to taste

Grate or shred the cabbage. Slice the onion very thinly. Mix the cabbage with all the other ingredients. Serve with rice and curry.

CURRIED COTTAGE CHEESE SALAD

METRIC/IMPERIAL

225 g/8 oz onions
1 teaspoon salt
2 tablespoons desiccated coconut
4 tablespoons hot milk
½ green pepper
12 sprigs green coriander or watercress
450 g/1 lb cottage cheese
juice of 2 lemons
¼ teaspoon freshly ground pepper

Peel and slice onions thinly crosswise. Sprinkle with ½ teaspoon salt and rub in with hands. Let stand for 30 minutes, then pour cold water over and drain well. Soak the coconut in hot milk and let stand for 30 minutes. Chop the green pepper and coriander or watercress sprigs coarsely. Mix everything together, adding remaining salt, and stir well. Set aside for 30 minutes after mixing. Serve cold.

ONION SALAD (1)

METRIC/IMPERIAL

4 large onions
¼ green pepper
4 teaspoons coriander or watercress leaves
5-mm/¼-inch piece fresh ginger
1 teaspoon salt
450 ml/¾ pint thick coconut milk (see page 17)

Peel and slice the onions finely. Chop the green pepper finely. Chop the leaves finely. Peel and chop ginger finely. Mix all ingredients together with salt and coconut milk and serve cold.

ONION SALAD (2)

METRIC/IMPERIAL

450 g/1 lb large onions
1 tomato
¼ cucumber
2 tablespoons coriander leaves
1 green chilli
4 teaspoons sugar
½ teaspoon salt
50 g/2 oz garlic vinegar

Peel and slice onions thinly. Peel and chop finely tomato and cucumber. Chop coriander leaves finely. Seed chilli and chop finely. Mix the sugar and salt in vinegar and dissolve. Put onions, cucumber and chilli into glass dish. Mix well and let soak in the mixed vinegar. Add the tomato before serving. Mix well and sprinkle with chopped coriander leaves. This is eaten with Dhansak.

BANANA AND COCONUT SALAD

METRIC/IMPERIAL

3 bananas
1 tablespoon desiccated coconut
2 tablespoons hot milk

Peel and slice bananas thinly. Soak coconut in hot milk for 30 minutes. Put slices of bananas in glass dish. Pour the soaked coconut milk over the slices and serve cold.

SPICED BANANA SALAD

METRIC/IMPERIAL

1 teaspoon butter
1 teaspoon cummin seeds
2 bananas
150 ml/¼ pint yogurt
1 teaspoon salt
¼ teaspoon chilli powder

Heat the butter gently in a saucepan. Fry the cummin seeds first. Then put in the peeled and mashed bananas, yogurt, salt and chilli powder. Stir all together. Take off heat and serve hot or cold. This is very good with pulaos.

CUCUMBER AND YOGURT SALAD

METRIC/IMPERIAL

1 large cucumber
300 ml/½ pint yogurt
50 g/2 oz desiccated coconut
2 tablespoons hot milk
¼ green pepper
15 g/½ oz butter
1 teaspoon black mustard seeds
1 teaspoon salt

Peel and grate the cucumber. Beat the yogurt till thick. Soak the coconut in the hot milk for 30 minutes. Chop the green pepper finely. Heat the butter in a small saucepan and fry the mustard seeds. When the seeds begin to burst add them to the yogurt together with the butter. Stir in all the other ingredients with the yogurt. Mix well and serve cold.

This is especially good with pulaos.

PUMPKIN AND MUSTARD SALAD

METRIC/IMPERIAL

225 g/8 oz pumpkin
¼ green pepper
½ teaspoon dry mustard
¼ teaspoon ginger powder
½ teaspoon cummin powder
½ teaspoon salt
150 ml/¼ pint yogurt

Peel and slice pumpkin. Chop green pepper very finely. Boil pumpkin, drain and keep warm. Mix mustard, ginger, cummin, salt and green pepper in the yogurt. Add the pumpkin. Mix well and serve.

This dish can be varied by using marrow, sliced bananas, tomatoes, cucumbers, boiled cauliflower sprigs or boiled slices of cabbage instead of pumpkin. Add or subtract the quantity of mustard to taste.

Chutneys and Pickles

Chutneys and pickles form an accompaniment to the main courses of a meal, but, unlike raitas and salads, are eaten in small quantities, to add just a slight extra touch of piquancy.

The most popular chutneys in India are freshly made of onion or coriander leaves or fresh mint. Pickles differ from chutneys in as much as they are made to be stored, and do not spoil with keeping, as do fresh chutneys.

APPLE CHUTNEY

METRIC/IMPERIAL

small piece green ginger or ¼ teaspoon ginger powder
225 g/8 oz onions
2 cloves garlic
1 kg/2 lb cooking apples
225 g/8 oz brown sugar
600 ml/1 pint malt vinegar
100 g/4 oz sultanas
15 g/½ oz mustard seeds
7 g/¼ oz salt
4 green chillies, chopped or 1 teaspoon chilli powder

Scrape the green ginger and grind or mince with onions and garlic. Peel and chop the apples. Cook the apples and sugar in the vinegar till the apples are soft. Cool. Add all the other ingredients and after bringing to the boil simmer for 15 minutes or till the mixture is thick and pulpy. Cool and bottle.

BENGAL APPLE CHUTNEY

METRIC/IMPERIAL

50 g/2 oz fresh ginger or 2 teaspoons ginger powder
1.75 litres/3 pints malt vinegar
100 g/4 oz onions
50 g/2 oz garlic cloves
16 large cooking apples
450 g/1 lb brown sugar
50 g/2 oz mustard seeds
1 tablespoon salt
15 g/½ oz chilli powder
225 g/8 oz raisins

Scrape ginger and wash in a little vinegar. Mince the ginger, onions and garlic. Peel and slice the apples. Boil the apples and sugar in the vinegar till the apples are soft. Add all the other ingredients and simmer for 15–20 minutes. Use a wooden spoon while cooking and stir often. Cool and bottle.

FRESH APPLE CHUTNEY

METRIC/IMPERIAL

50 g/2 oz desiccated coconut
4 tablespoons hot milk
25 g/1 oz salt
2 large green apples
2 tablespoons chopped onion
¼ green pepper or dash cayenne pepper
juice of 1 lemon

Soak desiccated coconut in hot milk for 20 minutes. Dissolve the salt in a bowl of cold water. Peel, core and chop the apples, put in cold salt water and leave for 10 minutes. Drain the apples and mix carefully with the onion. Chop the pepper finely or use the cayenne pepper. Mix all other ingredients together with the drained, soaked coconut. Put in glass dish, sprinkle with lemon juice, toss and serve.

TOMATO CHUTNEY (1)

METRIC/IMPERIAL

1.75 kg/4 lb tomatoes
50 g/2 oz garlic cloves
25 g/1 oz chilli powder
15 g/½ oz ginger powder
1 tablespoon salt
600 ml/1 pint malt vinegar
450 g/1 lb sugar
225 g/8 oz raisins

Skin tomatoes by plunging them into boiling water for 2 minutes. Cut into quarters. Chop the garlic very finely. Cook tomatoes, garlic, chilli, ginger and salt till the tomatoes are pulpy. Add the vinegar, sugar and raisins and cook till the mixture is thick. Cool and bottle.

TOMATO CHUTNEY (2)

METRIC/IMPERIAL

1.25 kg/2½ lb green tomatoes
4 green peppers
225 g/8 oz onions
7 g/¼ oz salt
750 ml/1¼ pints malt vinegar
225 g/8 oz brown sugar
7 g/¼ oz bruised green ginger
7 g/¼ oz cayenne pepper
7 g/¼ oz cloves
7 g/¼ oz mustard seeds

Slice the tomatoes and green peppers after washing. Peel and slice onions. Put tomatoes into large bowl in layers. Sprinkle each layer with salt and let stand overnight. Next morning drain the moisture. Place the tomatoes in a saucepan with the vinegar and all the other ingredients and simmer for 30 minutes. Remove from heat and strain. When cold pour into small bottles and keep in dry place. Use after a week as liked.

FRESH TOMATO CHUTNEY

METRIC/IMPERIAL

450 g/1 lb tomatoes
¼ green pepper
½ onion
¼ teaspoon salt
½ teaspoon sugar
15 g/½ oz garlic vinegar

Put tomatoes in boiling water for 2 minutes, then pour cold water over them and skin. Chop them. Chop the washed green pepper and the peeled onion. Mix with the tomatoes. Add salt, mix the sugar in the vinegar and sprinkle over all. Toss, put in glass dish and serve.

MINT CHUTNEY

METRIC/IMPERIAL

12 sprigs of mint
1 onion
½ green pepper
2 tablespoons desiccated coconut
2 tablespoons hot milk
175 ml/6 fl oz yogurt
½ teaspoon salt

Wash the mint. Peel the onion and halve. Wash the green pepper and dry. Chop all three very finely. Soak the coconut in the hot milk for 30 minutes. Beat yogurt till thin. Add salt. Mix all the ingredients well together. Serve cold.

This is specially good with pulaos.

FRESH MINT CHUTNEY

METRIC/IMPERIAL

50 g/2 oz mint leaves
1 small onion
2 green chillies
1 teaspoon sugar
salt to taste
lemon juice to taste

Wash the mint. Chop the onion and chillies. Grind the mint, onion and chillies. Add sugar, salt and lemon juice. Toss, put in glass dish and serve.

COCONUT CHUTNEY

METRIC/IMPERIAL

2 teaspoons desiccated coconut
2 tablespoons hot milk
3 cloves garlic
½ small onion
pinch of cayenne pepper
15 g/½ oz garlic vinegar

Soak coconut in hot milk for 30 minutes. Peel the garlic and onion and chop finely. Mix all the ingredients together well. Serve cold.

FRESH RED CHUTNEY

METRIC/IMPERIAL

3 dates
½ small onion
3 cloves garlic
¼ teaspoon chilli powder
½ teaspoon paprika
¼ teaspoon cummin powder
1 teaspoon salt
2 teaspoons malt vinegar

Stone the dates, peel and chop the onion and peel the garlic. Mince finely with all the other ingredients except the salt and vinegar, which should be mixed in well after mincing. Serve with vegetable fritters, or pakoras as they are called in northern India (see page 174).

GREEN GOOSEBERRY AMBAL

METRIC/IMPERIAL

1 walnut-size lump tamarind
225 g/8 oz gooseberries
1 tablespoon ghee
½ teaspoon mustard seeds
½ teaspoon chilli powder
2 teaspoons sugar
1 tablespoon raisins
salt to taste

Soak tamarind in 300 ml/½ pint water for 15 minutes then squeeze out the juice and strain. Fry the gooseberries in the fat and drain. Fry the mustard seeds in the fat and when the seeds burst add the gooseberries, tamarind juice and all the other ingredients and cook till the fruit is soft.

This chutney is eaten in Bengal, where it is made with various kinds of vegetables and fruit.

FRESH GREEN CHUTNEY

METRIC/IMPERIAL

4 teaspoons desiccated coconut
2 teaspoons hot milk
½ green pepper
4 teaspoons coriander or watercress leaves
2 cloves garlic
1 teaspoon salt
1 teaspoon sugar
2 teaspoons malt vinegar
1 teaspoon cummin powder

Soak the coconut in the hot milk for 30 minutes. Chop the green pepper coarsely. Chop the coriander or watercress leaves finely. Chop the cloves of garlic finely. Dissolve the salt and sugar in the vinegar. Mix all the ingredients together and add the vinegar mixture. Toss and serve. The chutney should be fairly thick and dry.

HOT TOMATO SAUCE

METRIC/IMPERIAL

2 cloves garlic
1 onion
750 ml/1¼ pints tomato juice
2 tablespoons Worcestershire sauce
2 teaspoons sugar
1½ teaspoons chilli powder
dash Tabasco
25 g/1 oz butter
2 teaspoons flour
1 tablespoon tomato purée
salt to taste
2 tablespoons port

Crush cloves of garlic. Chop onion finely. Mix garlic, onion, tomato juice, Worcestershire sauce, sugar, chilli powder and Tabasco and simmer in a covered pan for 20 minutes. Then rub through a sieve. In a separate pan melt butter, mix in flour and add the tomato purée. Gradually add the spiced tomato juice, stirring all the time. When well blended and thick add salt to taste and port. Remove from heat. More port can be added if liked.

MANGO CHUTNEY

METRIC/IMPERIAL

6 medium green mangoes
salt to taste
4 cloves garlic
25 g/1 oz fresh ginger
6 large dried red chillies
600 ml/1 pint malt vinegar
50 g/2 oz almonds
350 g/12 oz sugar
100 g/4 oz raisins

Peel and slice mangoes and sprinkle with salt. Grind the garlic, ginger and chillies to a paste with a little vinegar. Blanch and chop the almonds. Boil the vinegar, add sugar and mangoes and cook for 5 minutes over a low heat. Add the garlic, ginger and chilli paste and cook for 10 minutes. Add the almonds, raisins and more salt to taste and cook for 5 minutes more. Cool and bottle.

AMBACALIA

METRIC/IMPERIAL

2 large onions
225 g/8 oz small onions
1 (415-g/15-oz) can mango slices
450 g/1 lb gaur (Indian molasses)
50 g/2 oz butter
1 teaspoon ginger powder
½ teaspoon garlic salt
½ teaspoon salt

Peel and slice the large onions. Peel small onions and keep whole. Drain syrup from tin of mangoes and set aside. Crumble Indian molasses into 600 ml/1 pint water and add mango syrup. Heat the molasses and syrup water till molasses is dissolved. Strain and heat again. When hot, add the small whole onions and cook gently till done.

Heat the butter and fry the sliced onions till light brown, then add the ginger, garlic salt and salt and fry for 5 minutes more. Combine the fried onions with the small onions and mango slices. Stir well and simmer for 5 minutes more. Remove from heat and serve with Dhansak or any other dish.

SULTANA CHUTNEY

METRIC/IMPERIAL

675 g/1½ lb sultanas
50 g/2 oz fresh ginger
50 g/2 oz garlic cloves
25 g/1 oz almonds
450 ml/¾ pint malt vinegar
350 g/12 oz soft brown sugar
50 g/2 oz salt
7 g/¼ oz dried red chillies

Wash the sultanas, peel the ginger and cut in thin slices. Cut garlic cloves in thin slices. Blanch the almonds and remove skin. Soak the sultanas in the vinegar for 24 hours. Then mix all the ingredients in a saucepan, and bring to the boil. Simmer uncovered until vinegar is the consistency of syrup. Remove from heat and let it get quite cold. Bottle and cork.

This can be eaten the next day.

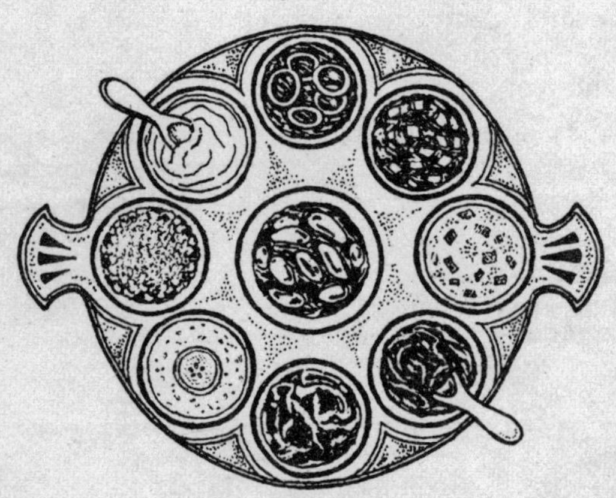

TOMATO AND HORSERADISH CHUTNEY

METRIC/IMPERIAL

450 g/1 lb green tomatoes
8 onions
12 whole long red chillies
50 g/2 oz salt
450 g/1 lb brown sugar
450 g/1 lb grated horseradish
2 tablespoons ground cinnamon
2 tablespoons ground cloves
600 ml/1 pint malt vinegar

Wash, wipe, and slice tomatoes. Peel and slice onions. Put tomatoes, onions and chillies alternately in a bowl and sprinkle salt on each layer. Leave overnight with a weight on to remove all moisture. Drain off moisture in the morning.

Put the tomatoes, onions and chillies into a saucepan with sugar, grated horseradish and ground cinnamon and cloves. Pour in the vinegar and simmer for 24 hours. Cool well.

Bottle tightly and use after 3 months.

RAISIN CHUTNEY

METRIC/IMPERIAL

- 50 g/2 oz tamarind
- ½ teaspoon turmeric
- ½ teaspoon chilli powder
- sugar and salt to taste
- 2 tablespoons mustard oil
- 1 teaspoon mustard seeds
- 2 green chillies, chopped
- 225 g/8 oz raisins

Soak tamarind in 150 ml/¼ pint water for 1 hour, then squeeze the tamarind into the same water and strain through fine sieve. Mix tamarind juice, turmeric, chilli, sugar and salt together. Heat the mustard oil and when smoking put in the mustard seeds and 1 chopped green chilli. Fry for 1 minute, lower heat and add the tamarind mixture. Cover the pan and as soon as the mixture begins to bubble add the raisins and boil till thick. Cool and bottle.

TOMATO, DATE AND RAISIN CHUTNEY

Oven temperature: Moderate
180°C, 350°F, Gas Mark 4

METRIC/IMPERIAL

- 1 kg/2 lb tomatoes
- 225 g/8 oz raisins
- 450 g/1 lb dates
- 100 g/4 oz garlic cloves
- 225 g/8 oz green ginger
- 2 tablespoons chilli powder
- juice of 2 lemons
- 450 g/1 lb brown sugar
- generous litre/2 pints malt vinegar

Wash and wipe tomatoes. Stone the raisins and dates. Peel cloves of garlic. Peel green ginger and slice. Bake the tomatoes in a baking tin in the oven and when soft mash the skin, seeds and pulp. Mince raisins, dates, ginger and garlic with the chilli powder. Mix the lemon juice with the minced ingredients. Boil the sugar with the vinegar gently till dissolved. Mix minced ingredients and mashed tomatoes into the sugar and vinegar and simmer for 2 hours uncovered. When liquid is reduced to less than half, remove from heat and allow to get quite cold. Bottle and cork.

Use after a fortnight.

PLUM CHUTNEY

METRIC/IMPERIAL

100 g/4 oz green ginger	1 kg/2 lb plums
50 g/2 oz garlic cloves	25 g/1 oz chilli powder
50 g/2 oz onion seeds	1 kg/2 lb sugar
25 g/1 oz mustard seeds	50 g/2 oz salt
600 ml/1 pint malt vinegar	

Grind the ginger, garlic, onion and mustard seeds to a paste in a little vinegar. Stone the plums. Cook the plums and all the other ingredients in the vinegar until thick and pulpy. Cool and bottle.

TOMATO KASAUNDI

METRIC/IMPERIAL

75 g/3 oz mustard seeds	600 ml/1 pint mustard or sweet oil
225 g/8 oz green ginger	25 g/1 oz turmeric
600 ml/1 pint malt vinegar	75 g/3 oz cummin powder
100 g/4 oz garlic cloves	50 g/2 oz chilli powder
50 g/2 oz green chillies	450 g/1 lb sugar
1.75 kg/4 lb tomatoes	50–75 g/2–3 oz salt

Grind the mustard seeds to a powder. Scrape the ginger and grind it with a little vinegar. Slice the garlic very finely. Cut the green chillies in half lengthwise. Wash, dry and chop the tomatoes. Heat the oil till it is smoking, then cool a little, add all the ground and powdered spices and fry over a low heat till the raw smell disappears. Add the tomatoes, garlic, chillies, vinegar, sugar and salt. Add only 50 g/2 oz salt at first and if more is required add it later. Cook on a low heat till the oil floats on top. Cool and bottle.

Let the pickle mature for a week before use.

BOMBAY DUCK CHUTNEY

METRIC/IMPERIAL

9–10 dried Bombay ducks
3 onions
2 cloves garlic
¼ teaspoon chilli powder
¼ teaspoon turmeric
15 g/½ oz desiccated coconut soaked in 1 tablespoon hot water
50 g/2 oz cooking fat
1 teaspoon salt

Remove bones from Bombay ducks, toast and crush. Slice onions. Chop garlic finely. Pound the garlic, chilli, turmeric and soaked coconut together well. Heat the cooking fat and fry the onions till medium brown. Put in the pounded mixture, salt and dry fish and fry gently till the fat nearly evaporates and the mixture is the consistency of breadcrumbs. Eat with brown bread and butter or use as a sandwich filling.

TOMATO KETCHUP

METRIC/IMPERIAL

1.5 kg/3 lb tomatoes
50 g/2 oz salt
600 ml/1 pint malt vinegar
50 g/2 oz brown sugar
2 teaspoons dry mustard
2 teaspoons ginger powder
2 teaspoons allspice
1 teaspoon black pepper

Wash the tomatoes and chop coarsely. Sprinkle with the salt and let them stand for 4 hours. Then boil in the vinegar for 30 minutes with the sugar, mustard, ginger, allspice and pepper. Allow the mixture to cool. Strain it well, bottle and cork. Use after 3 days.

LEMONS PICKLED IN SALT

Oven temperature: Cool
140°C, 275°F, Gas Mark 1

METRIC/IMPERIAL

450 g/1 lb lemons
100 g/4 oz green ginger
100 g/4 oz green chillies
575 g/1¼ lb rock salt
100 g/4 oz chilli powder

Wash and dry the lemons. Scrape the ginger, wash, then dry thoroughly and slice into thin slivers. Wash and dry the chillies and slice in half lengthwise. Put the salt and chilli powder into a bowl. Mix the ginger and chillies into the salt. Cut the lemons into quarters without severing them. Put the lemons into the bowl and rub them with the salt mixture. Have clean dry bottles ready and as each lemon is coated put it into a bottle. When all the lemons have been put into the bottles add all the remaining salt and cover the bottles.

This pickle should be put in the sun for two or three weeks but if it is not possible to do this put in the oven for the whole day. I have done so myself and the result has been good. The pickle will be ready to eat in about 2 months' time. This pickle is a great favourite in India and is said to have medicinal value when very old.

AUBERGINE PICKLE

METRIC/IMPERIAL

25 g/1 oz green ginger
2 cloves garlic
600 ml/1 pint vinegar
2 tablespoons chilli powder
2 teaspoons turmeric
2 teaspoons ginger powder
1.75 kg/4 lb aubergines
100 g/4 oz green chillies
300 ml/½ pint sesame or groundnut oil
2 teaspoons cummin seeds
2 teaspoons fenugreek seeds
3 tablespoons salt
225 g/8 oz sugar

Scrape the ginger and cut into small pieces. Slice 1 clove of garlic finely. Grind the other clove of garlic with a little vinegar and add the chilli powder, turmeric and ginger. Make into a paste. Wash and dry the aubergines and the green chillies. Cut into 2.5-cm/1-inch pieces. Heat oil till it is smoking. Cool, put in the cummin and fenugreek seeds and fry for 1 minute. Add the sliced garlic and when brown add the paste and fry over a low heat till the paste smells cooked and the oil floats on top. Add the rest of the vinegar, then salt and sugar and mix thoroughly. Add the aubergines, chillies and ginger and boil till the oil floats on top. Taste, and if more salt is required add while hot. Cool and bottle.

Leave for a fortnight before using.

DRY FISH PICKLE

METRIC/IMPERIAL

1 kg/2 lb dried white fish
150 ml/¼ pint sweet oil
150 ml/¼ pint vinegar
50 g/2 oz tamarind
50 g/2 oz dry mustard
8 cloves garlic
25 g/1 oz chilli powder
1 teaspoon turmeric
1 tablespoon cummin seeds or powder
1 teaspoon salt

Cut the dried fish (haddock is very good for this) into slices 1 cm/½ inch thick crosswise. Soak the fish steaks in cold water to cover for 1 hour. Remove from water, wash well and dry thoroughly. Heat the sweet oil to very hot. Lower heat to medium, put in the fish slices till well browned, then remove and let the fish cool. In half the vinegar soak the tamarind for 1 hour, then rub well into the vinegar, strain and set aside. Pour the other half of the vinegar on to the dry mustard and mix well. Chop the cloves of garlic finely. Mix the garlic, chilli, turmeric, cummin seeds or powder and salt with the mustard vinegar.

Pour in the strained thickish tamarind vinegar and mix well. Coat all the fish slices with the mixture and leave to stand for 1 hour, then put in a large glass jar and cork well.

It will be ready in a fortnight. Eat this pickle with white rice and lightly fried dal. Any dried white fish may be treated this way.

GREEN PEPPER PICKLE

METRIC/IMPERIAL

450 g/1 lb green peppers
450 g/1 lb green tomatoes
8 onions
100 g/4 oz salt
575 g/1¼ lb brown sugar
2 tablespoons ground cloves
2 tablespoons ground cinnamon
900 ml/1½ pints vinegar

Wash and dry the green peppers and tomatoes. Slice them. Peel and slice the onions finely. Sprinkle green peppers, tomatoes and onion slices with the salt. Put a weight on them and let stand all night. Next morning drain off the moisture. Put in a saucepan and add the sugar and ground spices. Cover with the vinegar and simmer the mixture for 12 hours. Let the mixture get quite cold.

Bottle and keep for a week before using.

PICKLED NASTURTIUM SEEDS

METRIC/IMPERIAL

675 g/1½ lb nasturtium seeds
100 g/4 oz onions
7 g/¼ oz dried red chillies
15 g/½ oz ground mace
15 g/½ oz cloves
600 ml/1 pint white wine vinegar

Soak the nasturtium seeds in cold salted water for 4 whole days, changing the solution every day. Slice the onions and the dried red chillies crosswise. Boil the spices, onions and chillies in the vinegar. Fill glass jars with the seeds. Pour the heated vinegar and spices in each jar and cover.

Use after 3 months.

PLAIN PEACH PICKLE

METRIC/IMPERIAL

1 kg/2 lb peaches
6 ml/1 pint vinegar
450 g/1 lb soft brown sugar
50 g/2 oz cinnamon sticks
50 g/2 oz cloves

Choose nearly ripe peaches and, without peeling, put them into a large earthenware jar. Pour the vinegar into a saucepan and add the sugar, cinnamon and cloves and let them simmer gently together for 1 hour. While hot pour this mixture over the peaches. Lay a weight on top to keep the peaches submerged. Leave for 3 days. Then put mixture and peaches into a large saucepan and boil till the peaches are soft. Take the peaches carefully from the syrup and pack into clean jars. Boil up the syrup again and quickly pour it over the peaches in the jars. Cork and seal while hot.

Eat after 8 days. This pickle is specially good with cold meats and boiled potatoes.

SWEETENED HOT PLUM PICKLE

METRIC/IMPERIAL

1 kg/2 lb plums
225 g/8 oz raisins
50 g/2 oz garlic cloves
50 g/2 oz fresh ginger
100 g/4 oz almonds
7 g/¼ oz chilli powder
50 g/2 oz mustard seeds
900 ml/1½ pints vinegar
575 g/1¼ lb brown sugar

Choose firm, nearly ripe plums. Wash and dry them. Seed the raisins. Peel the garlic. Peel the fresh ginger and cut into matchstick size slices. Blanch and skin the almonds. Pound slightly the raisins, garlic, fresh ginger, almonds, chilli powder and mustard seeds in a little vinegar. Stone the plums and put with the other ingredients, sugar and remaining vinegar into a saucepan and stew or simmer for 24 hours on a very low heat, keeping tightly covered. Remove from heat after 24 hours and let get quite cold.

Bottle and cork and use after 6 months.

HOT AND SWEET APPLE PICKLE

Oven temperature: Cool
140°C, 275°F, Gas Mark 1

METRIC/IMPERIAL

24 large unripe apples
100 g/4 oz fresh ginger
225 g/8 oz raisins
50 g/2 oz garlic cloves
100 g/4 oz white mustard seeds
1.75 litres/3 pints vinegar
450 g/1 lb soft brown sugar
100 g/4 oz salt
50 g/2 oz shallots
50 g/2 oz dried red chillies

Choose large green unripe apples. Peel, core and slice them. Peel the fresh ginger and slice into matchstick size slices. Wash and remove pips from raisins. Slice cloves of garlic. Wash the mustard seeds in a little vinegar and dry out in the oven. Dissolve the sugar in a generous litre/2 pints vinegar, then add the sliced apples and raisins, and boil together until the apples are tender and soft. Allow the mixture to get quite cold, then add all the other ingredients including the mustard seeds, ginger and garlic, as well as the remaining 600 ml/1 pint vinegar. Mix well and simmer for 45 minutes. Remove from heat and allow mixture to get quite cold. Stir well, then bottle and cork tightly. Eat after 4 days.

HOT PEACH PICKLE

METRIC/IMPERIAL

1 kg/2 lb peaches	225 g/8 oz sultanas
450 g/1 lb brown sugar	25 g/1 oz chilli powder
600 ml/1 pint vinegar	1 teaspoon ginger powder

Choose nearly ripe peaches and blanch them in very hot water. Remove the skins. Split them open with a silver knife and extract the stones. Boil the sugar in half the vinegar. While the vinegar is boiling hot, drop in the peach halves. Simmer until they are quite soft, then add the sultanas, chilli, ginger and the remaining vinegar. Reduce the liquid to desired thickness. Remove from heat, stir well. Let it become quite cold. Bottle and cork and eat after 15 days.

MINCED LEMON PICKLE

METRIC/IMPERIAL

1 kg/2 lb lemons	1 teaspoon chilli powder
50 g/2 oz salt	2 teaspoons ginger powder
450 g/1 lb seeded raisins	900 ml/1½ pints vinegar
25 g/1 oz garlic cloves	675 g/1½ lb soft brown sugar

Cut the lemons in quarters, remove the pips and soak with salt in a bowl for 4 days, stirring often. Soak the raisins, garlic cloves, chilli and ginger for 24 hours in a little vinegar. Mince lemons and raisin mixture together. Add the sugar to the rest of the vinegar and mix well. Mix together, put in a saucepan and bring to the boil then simmer till liquid is reduced and thickened. Let it get quite cold, then bottle. This pickle can be eaten after 4 days.

Desserts

There are hundreds of different varieties of sweets in India, some more characteristic of one part than another but all of them equally popular everywhere when available. Typical Bengali sweets are rasgullas, rasmolai and gulab jamun (milk sweets). In the north jalebi (milk sweets) and barfi (a kind of milk-based fudge) are typical. There are also various kinds of halvas, prepared from vegetables, fruits, nuts and eggs.

Most of the best sweets and halvas are complicated and take a long time to prepare, therefore many people buy instead of making them.

VERMICELLI KHEER

METRIC/IMPERIAL

100 g/4 oz fine vermicelli
generous litre/2 pints rich or unpasteurized milk
100 g/4 oz sugar
25 g/1 oz butter or ghee
25 g/1 oz raisins
25 g/1 oz blanched almonds
pinch of cardamom powder

In a dry frying pan, roast the vermicelli till lightly browned. Add vermicelli to the milk in a saucepan and bring to the boil. Boil steadily till the vermicelli is tender, then add the sugar and remove from the heat when the sugar has dissolved. Melt butter and fry the raisins and blanched almonds and add to the kheer. Sprinkle with cardamom powder.

Serve hot or cold.

ZARDA

(Sweet Rice)

Oven temperature: Cool
150°C, 300°F, Gas Mark 2

METRIC/IMPERIAL

10 almonds
50 g/2 oz raisins
4 cardamoms
450 g/1 lb rice
50 g/2 oz ghee or butter
½ teaspoon salt
small stick cinnamon
4 cloves
150 ml/¼ pint milk
100 g/4 oz sugar
¼ teaspoon saffron
2 teaspoons lemon juice

Blanch almonds and slice them. Wash the raisins and drain. Grind the cardamoms coarsely. Boil the rice in 3.5 litres/6 pints water and drain when half cooked.

In a large pan heat the ghee and fry the rice and salt for a few minutes. Add the cinnamon, cloves and the cardamoms with the milk (less 1 tablespoon) and sugar and cook till the rice is done. Soak the saffron in 1 tablespoon milk and add to the cooked rice. Add the raisins and the lemon juice and cook gently for 5 minutes.

Put the pan in the oven or turn the rice into a casserole, cover and put in the oven for 10 minutes. Serve garnished with almonds.

SEMOLINA HALVA

METRIC/IMPERIAL

100 g/4 oz sugar
100 g/4 oz ghee or unsalted butter
100 g/4 oz semolina
25 g/1 oz blanched almonds, sliced
25 g/1 oz raisins
2 cardamoms, coarsely ground (optional)

Boil 600 ml/1 pint water and the sugar till the sugar is dissolved. Heat the ghee and fry the semolina in a large saucepan, stirring all the time. Just before the semolina is fried thoroughly, add the blanched sliced almonds and the raisins and fry. Very carefully add the sugar syrup to the fried semolina and stir. Cook till the halva is a thick consistency and leaves the sides of the pan.

Coarsely ground cardamoms may also be added if liked.

PARSEE CUSTARD

Oven temperature: Hot
220°C, 425°F, Gas Mark 7

METRIC/IMPERIAL

900 ml/1½ pints rich or unpasteurized milk
50 g/2 oz castor sugar
5 eggs
1 tablespoon ground almonds
1 tablespoon rose water
pinch grated nutmeg and cardamom powder

Boil the milk and sugar together on a low heat till the quantity has been reduced by half. Allow to cool a little and add 3 whole eggs plus 2 egg yolks, well beaten together. Add the almonds and rose water. Put the custard into an ovenproof dish and sprinkle with the nutmeg and cardamom.

Place the dish in a pan of hot water. Bake for 45 minutes to 1 hour in the oven, till the custard is set.

This sweet is eaten at Parsee weddings.

MOTI CHOOR LADDU

METRIC/IMPERIAL

100 g/4 oz gram flour
175 g/6 oz sugar
few strands saffron
2 green cardamoms, ground
50 g/2 oz almonds, blanched and sliced
450 g/1 lb ghee or vegetable fat

Mix the gram flour with water to make a thick paste and beat thoroughly. Make a syrup with the sugar and 300 ml/½ pint water. Cook till stringy, then put in the saffron, ground in warm water, the ground cardamoms and the almonds.

In a large deep frying pan melt the ghee. The boondis are made by putting some of the gram mixture on a ladle with small holes and shaking it over the hot fat: the mixture will fall through the holes like small pearls. Fry these till they are golden brown and crisp. Put them in the syrup as soon as they are drained. When all the boondis are ready and mixed in the syrup, grease your hands and form into small balls the size of an apple.

MYSORE PAK

METRIC/IMPERIAL

100 g/4 oz gram flour
275 g/10 oz sugar
350–450 g/12 oz–1lb ghee

Sift the gram flour. Make a syrup of the sugar in 150 ml/¼ pint water and boil for 5 minutes, when it should be sticky.

Melt 100 g/4 oz ghee and fry the gram flour in it, stirring all the time. Add the syrup and keep stirring. Put the rest of the ghee into another pan and bring to simmering point. Put into a jug and dribble it on to the gram flour which must be stirred all the time. Continue frying for 10 minutes then pour on to a flat greased surface to set.

Mysore Pak quickly becomes hard so should be cut into desired shapes immediately.

GULAB JAMUN

METRIC/IMPERIAL

100 g/4 oz dried milk
2 tablespoons plain flour
pinch of bicarbonate of soda
4–5 tablespoons milk
225 g/8 oz vegetable fat for frying
450 g/1 lb sugar
2 cardamoms
rose water for flavouring

Mix the dried milk, flour and bicarbonate of soda in a bowl. Add fresh milk to make a smooth soft dough; make thin 2-inch long rolls.

Heat the fat, then cool and put over a low heat. Put in as many rolls as the pan will hold comfortably. Cook over a very low heat till the jamuns are a pale gold and have swollen to twice their size. In the meantime put the sugar and 300 ml/½ pint water in a large pan and make a thick syrup. Add the cardamoms, either coarsely ground or whole, to the syrup. Drain the jamuns and add to the syrup. The syrup should be kept over a low heat after adding the jamuns. When all the jamuns are in the syrup, leave for 5 minutes then take off the heat and add 1 tablespoon rose water and cool. The above quantity makes two dozen jamuns.

These may be eaten hot or cold.

ALMOND BARFI

METRIC/IMPERIAL

100 g/4 oz castor sugar
50 g/2 oz butter
225 g/8 oz ground almonds

Make a syrup with the sugar and 3 tablespoons water. Boil till it is stringy. Take off the heat, add the butter and almonds and pour very quickly and thinly on to a marble slab or greased plate. Flatten and cut into diamond shapes.

SANDESH

METRIC/IMPERIAL

2.25 litres/4 pints rich or unpasteurized milk
juice of 1 lemon
175 g/6 oz castor or icing sugar
1 green cardamom, coarsely ground

Boil the milk and add the lemon juice. Stir till the milk curdles. Take off the heat and strain the milk through muslin. Do not throw away all the whey. Hang up the thick curds in another piece of muslin and let it drip. When all the liquid has dripped out of the curds, put the curd in a bowl and knead it well or put on to a smooth board and break it up with a pastry roller till smooth. Put the curds (cheese) in a heavy frying pan and fry till warm. If the cheese is too dry a little whey may be added. Add the sugar and keep frying till it hardens. Spread on a flat dish and sprinkle with the coarsely ground cardamom. Cut into squares when cool.

GRAM MATHAI

METRIC/IMPERIAL

450 g/1 lb gram flour
225 g/8 oz ghee
450 g/1 lb castor sugar
chopped almonds, walnuts or pistachio nuts

Fry the gram flour in the ghee till a light brown, stirring all the time. Remove from the heat and mix in the sugar and nuts. Spread on a plate and cut into small squares when set.

MALPUA

METRIC/IMPERIAL

generous litre/2 pints rich or unpasteurized milk
75 g/3 oz sugar
50 g/2 oz flour
225 g/8 oz ghee

Boil the milk and simmer, stirring often till the milk has thickened and is about half its original quantity. Make a syrup with the sugar and 300 ml/½ pint water. Put this syrup in the dish in which the sweet will be served.

Mix the flour and milk and stir the batter well; it should be the consistency of pancake batter. Heat the ghee, pour 1 tablespoon batter into it and fry over low heat. When one side is done turn over, and when golden brown take out and drain; put each into the syrup as it is done.

KHATAI
(Biscuits)

Oven temperature: Moderately hot
190°C, 375°F, Gas Mark 5

METRIC/IMPERIAL

100 g/4 oz flour
175 g/6 oz sugar
75 g/3 oz semolina
100 g/4 oz ghee or butter

Mix all the ingredients and knead into a pliable dough. Make into small balls and bake in the oven till golden brown.

RASAGULLA

METRIC/IMPERIAL

generous litre/2 pints rich or unpasteurized milk
juice of 1 large lemon
2 teaspoons semolina
2–3 green cardamoms
450 g/1 lb sugar

Boil the milk and add the lemon juice. Stir and, when the milk curdles, remove from the heat. Cool. Strain through a clean cloth. Do not squeeze but hang it up as for jelly and let the whey drip. Leave overnight if possible. Put the cheese in a bowl, add the semolina and knead till the cheese is smooth. The smoother the cheese the better the sweet. Peel the cardamoms and keep the seeds. Take a piece of cheese paste the size of a walnut and roll into a ball. Make a dent in the centre; put in one or two cardamom seeds, close around them and make into a smooth round ball. Make as many balls as you can out of the paste. Make a thin syrup with the sugar and 1.75 litres/3 pints water, bring to the boil and put in one ball. If the ball does not break put in all the others and boil slowly till the balls are cooked.

They should become nearly double their original size and float on the surface of the syrup.

JALEBIS

METRIC/IMPERIAL

15 g/½ oz yeast
450 g/1 lb flour
pinch of saffron
2 tablespoons yogurt
450 g/1 lb sugar
1 teaspoon rose water
vegetable fat for frying

Dissolve the yeast in 150 ml/¼ pint warm water. Sift the flour and add enough water with the yeast liquid to make a thick batter. Grind the saffron and soak in 2 teaspoons warm water. Add this to the batter. Beat the yogurt until smooth and add to the batter. Leave for 1 hour.

Make a syrup with the sugar and 600 ml/1 pint water, boiling until thick. Flavour with the rose water and keep warm.

Heat the fat in a frying pan and put some batter in a piping bag. Pipe round swirls of batter into the hot fat and fry on both sides till crisp. Drain and put into the syrup for 2 minutes. Remove and put in a dish.

COCONUT TOFFEE

METRIC/IMPERIAL

1 coconut
225 g/8 oz sugar
25 g/1 oz butter
1 teaspoon vanilla essence

Grate the coconut. Make a thick syrup with the sugar and 150 ml/¼ pint water. Bring to the boil, add the coconut and butter. Simmer for 5 minutes. Add the vanilla essence. Keep stirring all the time till the mixture starts leaving the sides of the pan. Pour on to a greased slab or plate and cut into squares when set.

COCONUT BARFI

METRIC/IMPERIAL

450 g/1 lb castor sugar
2 green cardamoms
few strands saffron
450 g/1 lb freshly grated coconut
450 g/1 lb dried milk

Heat the sugar with 150 ml/¼ pint water. Peel and grind the cardamoms. Soak the saffron in a little water. When the syrup is ready, add the coconut and dried milk and mix thoroughly. Put on the heat and when the mixture begins to thicken add the saffron and the ground cardamom. Grease a slab or plate and pour the coconut mixture on to it. Cut into squares when set.

PISTACHIO BARFI

METRIC/IMPERIAL

225 g/8 oz pistachios	450 g/1 lb castor sugar
225 g/8 oz dried milk	rose water

Soak the pistachios in boiling water and remove their skins. Grind to a paste. Add the dried milk.

Make a syrup of the sugar and 150 ml/¼ pint water, bring to the boil and add the pistachio and dried milk mixture. Stir all the time while cooking. When the mixture becomes thick and is of setting consistency, pour on to a greased slab or plate. Flatten out with a roller and sprinkle with rose water. Cut into squares when set.

BANANA HALVA OR CONSERVE

METRIC/IMPERIAL

6 ripe bananas
15 g/½ oz melted butter
175 g/6 oz sugar
15 g/½ oz almonds, blanched
15 g/½ oz ground almonds
1 teaspoon vanilla essence
½ teaspoon mixed grated nutmeg and cardamom powder

Peel the bananas, slit in half and cut into 3 pieces each. Heat the melted butter and put in the bananas. Stir and add 2 tablespoons hot water. Cook till the bananas are a light cream colour; then mash and remove from heat. Make a thin syrup with the sugar and 300 ml/½ pint water, bring to the boil and add to the bananas. Cook together till the mixture is sticky. Then add the blanched and ground almonds and stir over a gentle heat until the mixture is soft like a ball of sticky toffee.

Remove from heat, add the vanilla essence and stir thoroughly.

Spread on a greased plate or marble slab and when cool cut into squares or diamonds and sprinkle with the mixed spice powders.

FLAT DATE CAKES

METRIC/IMPERIAL

500 g/18 oz dates
250 g/9 oz unsalted margarine or vegetable fat for frying
3 tablespoons milk
15 g/½ oz ground almonds
1 teaspoon rose water or vanilla essence
225 g/8 oz semolina
½ teaspoon salt
75 g/3 oz butter
225 g/8 oz self-raising flour

Stone the dates and fry in margarine. Remove from the heat and add the milk. Mash to a pulp and add the almonds and flavouring.

Sprinkle semolina with salt and add 1 teaspoon melted butter. Knead the semolina with ice cold water into a soft dough. Cream the rest of the butter and add flour to it gradually to form a very soft dough. Roll out the semolina dough into a thick round and spread the flour dough on it, keeping the edges clear. Pick up the edges of the semolina dough and take them into the centre, thus covering the flour dough. Roll into a ball and pull out into a long roll. Cut into 8 pieces. Divide the date mixture into 8 portions. Take a piece of dough and roll into a ball, depress the centre and fill with date mixture. Close by drawing dough over dates and flattening.

Fry in the margarine remaining in the pan till both sides are browned.

This is a delicious sweet and can be served with tea or after dinner.

INDIAN ALMOND FUDGE

METRIC/IMPERIAL

few strands saffron (optional)
225 g/8 oz sugar
225 g/8 oz plain flour
50 g/2 oz butter
25 g/1 oz ground almonds
25 g/1 oz ground walnuts or pistachios

If using saffron, toast and mix in 1 tablespoon hot water. Make a thin syrup with the sugar and 300 ml/½ pint water. Bring to the boil and add the flour. Cook, stirring all the time, till the mixture is thick. Add the butter, a little at a time. Keep stirring all the time and when the mixture starts leaving the sides of the pan, add the ground nuts and the saffron. Pour on to a greased marble slab or plate.

Cut into shapes before it is completely cold.

SEMOLINA FUDGE

METRIC/IMPERIAL

100 g/4 oz almonds
1 kg/2 lb castor sugar
450 g/1 lb fine semolina
450 g/1 lb butter
2 tablespoons rose water

Blanch and halve the almonds. Put sugar, 2½ tablespoons water and the semolina in a saucepan and cook over a moderate heat, stirring all the time till the mixture is thick.

Then add spoonfuls of butter, stirring constantly. When all the butter has been put in, add the almonds and rose water. Stir thoroughly, then pour on to a greased plate or marble slab. Cut into diamond shapes before it is completely cold.

CASHEW NUT FUDGE

METRIC/IMPERIAL

225 g/8 oz raw cashew nuts
25 g/1 oz walnuts
350 g/12 oz sugar
4 tablespoons rose water
225 g/8 oz butter
½ teaspoon salt
1 tablespoon hot milk

Mince or grind the cashew nuts. Grind the walnuts. Make a syrup with the sugar and 4 tablespoons water. Add the rose water to the ground cashew nuts and mix well. Put the cashew nut mixture into the syrup and cook, stirring all the time, till the mixture is thick. Add the butter gradually, a little at a time. Keep stirring and when the butter begins to come to the top add the walnuts, salt and milk and remove from the heat after 1 minute.

Pour on to a greased slab or plate and cut into diamond shapes before completely set.

KOPERAPAK
(Coconut Toffee)

METRIC/IMPERIAL

15 g/½ oz almonds
175 g/6 oz sugar
3 tablespoons rose water
50 g/2 oz desiccated coconut
½ teaspoon butter

Blanch and slice almonds thinly. In a saucepan put in the sugar, rose water, coconut and ½ teaspoon butter. Mix, then cook over a medium heat till all the liquid is gone. Spread at once on to a buttered slab or plate and sprinkle with the almond slices.

Allow to cool, then cut into square or diamond shapes.

ALMOND AND PEANUT TOFFEE

Oven temperature: Cool
140°C, 275°F, Gas Mark 1

METRIC/IMPERIAL

175 g/6 oz almonds
175 g/6 oz peanuts
9 tablespoons jaggery* or molasses
25 g/1 oz butter

* *Jaggery is sugar crystals coated lightly with molasses.*

Blanch almonds and peanuts. Split them in half. Dry them and put them in the oven till they are crisp and brown. Put the jaggery in a pan and melt over a very low heat. Do not add any water. When the jaggery is slightly tacky, add the almonds and peanuts and mix thoroughly. Grease a marble slab or a plate with butter and pour the mixture on it. Grease a rolling pin and roll out the toffee thinly. While still hot, cut into desired shapes.

Separate when cold and store in airtight jars.

MUSCAT HALVA

METRIC/IMPERIAL

350 g/12 oz plain flour
1.5 kg/3 lb sugar
300 ml/½ pint milk
1 tablespoon rose water
50 g/2 oz blanched almonds, sliced
225 g/8 oz ghee

Put the flour into a coarse cloth. Draw all the sides of the cloth together and tie firmly so that it will not open easily. Take a large bowl and put in the cloth with the flour. Add a little water and squeeze out the starch. Keep on squeezing till the water becomes thick. Keep this water aside and repeat the above with fresh water. Do this 4–5 times, using a total of a generous litre/2 pints water. The sticky substance left in the cloth can be thrown away.

To the starch water add the sugar. Put in a pan and boil, stirring all the time, till very thick. Add the milk, rose water and the blanched and sliced almonds. Add the ghee in spoonfuls. When the halva becomes transparent turn it on to a flat dish. Cut when cold.

Index

Poultry:

Pulses:

Rice:

Vegetables: